THROUGH THE
EYES OF **GOD**
UNDERSTANDING GOD'S PERSPECTIVE OF THE WORLD
JOHN MARSHALL

Randall House Publications
114 Bush Road • PO Box 17306
Nashville, TN 37217 USA
randallhouse.com

THROUGH THE EYES OF **GOD**
UNDERSTANDING GOD'S PERSPECTIVE OF THE WORLD
By John Marshall
Published by Randall House Publications
114 Bush Road
Nashville, Tennessee 37217

© Copyright 2005
Randall House Publications

All Scripture quotations, unless otherwise indicated, are
taken from *The Holy Bible*, King James Version. Those
marked NASB are taken from the *New American
Standard Bible*, © Copyright 1960, 1962, 1963, 1968,
1971, 1972, 1973, 1975, 1977, 1995 by the Lockman
Foundation. Used by permission. All rights reserved.

Printed in the United States of America
ISBN 0892655135

THROUGH THE
EYES OF **GOD**
UNDERSTANDING GOD'S PERSPECTIVE OF THE WORLD
JOHN MARSHALL

TABLE OF CONTENTS

*This book is dedicated to my wife
Ruth,
who shares with me the
journey, and makes it fun.*

JOHN MARSHALL "GETS IT!" I hope you "get it" too as you read *Through the Eyes of God*! In a day when Christian periodicals and books abound, it seems that few focus on the main thing. And what is that *main thing*? Dr. Paul Smith, noted pastor and global missions leader from the Peoples Church of Toronto, Canada used to say, "the main thing is to keep the main thing the main thing." The whole of Scripture reveals that the main thing is for God to be worshiped by all the people of the world. This is the overarching purpose of the church!

John Marshall rightly says there is only one purpose for the church—its overarching mission is to "declare His glory to the nations." At Global Focus, one of our favorite catch phrases is "the Bible is a God book, not a me book." Another favorite phrase is "worship is the primary motivation and ultimate culmination of missions." These phrases are supportive of the primary emphasis John makes.

This book is about an exciting journey in the life of a man of God and his local church. God placed a hunger in his heart to know the purpose of the church and how it should function. All the programs and paths prescribed to him in a lifetime of ministry did not satisfy that hunger. I was privileged to enter John and his church's journey early on in the process. I have never met a more eager man of God or a more eager group of church leaders. How my heart has been blessed to know them.

Their church is alive! They are properly motivated to declare His glory to the nations, and they are balanced in their approach. Jesus exhorted us to be His witnesses in "Jerusalem, Judea, Samaria and to the ends of the earth." Making contemporary, practical application of this strategy will keep a church moving in the right direction. They truly have a local and global approach. Acts 1:8 is their watchword! This has revolutionized them and set a pattern for hundreds of other pastors and churches.

You will be inspired, encouraged, and challenged as you read the story of this journey. It has been an exciting one to watch and to contribute to in some small way. This is a people and a man truly onboard with God's mission. They do what they do with excellence. They are motivated by biblical truth. They are energized by His Spirit. They are encouraged by the fruit of their labors. I hope you will be too!

Dr. Larry D. Reesor
Founder/President
Global Focus

"OF MAKING MANY BOOKS," Solomon said, "there is no end" (Ecclesiastes 12:14). This writing continues the legacy of proving the truth of Solomon's words.

Why another book? I have not written to provoke, pontificate, or be profound. My intent is to aid fellow believers on their pilgrimage, to help them fulfill their desire to come "unto the measure of the stature of the fullness of Christ" (Ephesians 4:13).

We need a broader perspective of the world. I pray this book will help the reader see the masses as Jesus sees them. May we see in the corner of His eye the tear which always lingers for the unreached peoples of the world. God grant us His perspective of the world. May we seek to reach to all the world, beginning next door.

Dr. John E. Marshall

CHAPTER 1

MORE THAN A SPECTATOR

"AND THIS GOSPEL OF THE KINGDOM SHALL BE PREACHED IN ALL THE WORLD
FOR A WITNESS UNTO ALL NATIONS; AND THEN SHALL THE END COME."

— **Matthew 24:14**

YEARS AGO my family received free tickets to a St. Louis Cardinals' baseball game. Upon entering Busch Stadium, ushers kept motioning us higher and higher up stairways, and farther and farther around the building. Finally, we arrived at our seats in dead center field, in the section farthest from home plate. We were so far away from the batter that we would see him swing at the ball, and then later hear the sound of the bat hitting it. We were too far away to see the ball's movement off the bat, and had to watch for running fielders to tell where the ball had headed. We were on the outskirts of the action, barely involved. The game was a distant reality, something way off in the distance.

That's how I felt a few years ago when the Lord began to burden my heart for worldwide missions. I felt as if I were way off in the bleachers somewhere. I could hear Jesus giving the Great Commission, but it seemed only a faint whisper, a barely audible echo. I was in the stadium, but the game was not a vital factor in my life.

I wondered how this could be. I am a sixth-generation preacher in one of the most mission-minded denominations in the history of Christianity. I have been in church my whole life. Preaching is all I have ever known. How could I have dabbled in missions through 30 years of ministry, but all of a sudden feel I was an outsider looking on?

To make my situation even more confusing, I believe I was not an exception to the rule, but rather typical of many of my generation (baby boomers) of preachers. We knew the ground rules. We learned how to play our part in supporting offerings and causes, but worldwide missions somehow never became hot on our hearts.

As the burden for missions grew heavier on my heart, I became curious. How did we reach such a low missions ebb at this point in time and history? My curiosity drove me to do research. I needed to know for my own peace of mind.

My concern about prioritizing kingdom advance is not merely an intellectual curiosity for me. It is a real life-and-blood issue, a matter of grave concern as I seek to understand the role we have in third millennium. I hope my personal struggle with prioritizing missions and evangelism will help others grappling with this issue.

The old adage is true, if you would understand anything, you must know its beginnings. With this in mind, I began my search to understand how many in my generation of godly, consecrated people had overlooked the burning drive for missions.

When I was in seminary (1972-75), we spent time discussing the purposes of the church. We compiled lists, usually naming fellowship, ministry, discipleship, worship, and missions/evangelism. Missions—sharing the gospel with those who are not prospects for our own local church, and evangelism—sharing the gospel with those who are, were combined to encompass the total outreach function of a local church.

We debated the relative importance of the items on this purpose list. The most vigorous discussions involved whether worship or missions/evangelism should top the list.

I submit for consideration a different scenario. Perhaps the church has only one overriding purpose—to help fulfill the mission of the kingdom of God. If this be the case, we would be more precise to discuss functions, not purposes (plural), needing to be done by the church to help accomplish her one overarching purpose.

I call attention to our Lord's definitive statement on the church. After Simon Peter's great confession that Jesus is "the Christ, the Son of the living God" (Matthew 16:16), our Master said, "Upon this rock I will build my church; and the gates of hell shall not prevail against it" (Matthew 16:18b).

While most churchgoers are acquainted with this famous passage, rarely can they recall what Jesus said next. Without stopping or hesitating, Christ continued, "And I will give unto thee the keys of the kingdom of heaven; and whatsoever thou shalt bind on earth shall be bound in heaven: and whatsoever thou shalt loose on earth shall be loosed in heaven" (Matthew 16:19).

With this pronouncement, Jesus forever wed the kingdom and the church. The kingdom, being the larger overarching entity entailing not only the church, but every manifestation of God's rule in the hearts of people, includes, for example, the calling of Abraham, the selection of Israel, the establishment of Judaism, and the inspiration of the Old Testament. Oppressed by Rome, the Israelites became obsessed with kingdom thinking and longed for the coming of an anointed king of David's family, who would politically rule over them and the world.

Into this environment Jesus came preaching, "The kingdom of heaven is at hand" (Matthew 4:17; also Mark 1:15 and Luke 4:43). He commanded His disciples to proclaim the exact same message, "As ye go, preach, saying, The kingdom of God is at hand" (Matthew 10:7; also Luke 9:2; 10:9). According to our text, Matthew 24:14, Jesus expects His followers in every era to continue preaching this theme until He returns.

Jesus' understanding of the kingdom was in line with, but not identified with what had become the main Jewish interpretation dealing with what God had intended from the beginning. Jesus introduced into human history the true messianic reign, the one prophets and holy writings had foretold.

By His own death, burial, resurrection, and ascension, He initiated "with power" (Mark 9:1) the final earthly phase of God's kingdom, that portion of the kingdom to be consummated in the great cataclysm when Jesus bodily returns to earth to rule over all things as King of kings and Lord of lords.

The kingdom of God, marching victoriously toward this climax, now encompasses the church, parachurch groups, seminaries, missions agencies, etc. Since these are all subsets of the kingdom, the overarching entity, each by its very nature has as its purpose to help fulfill the mission of the kingdom. Thus, any attempt to list accurately the proper functions of the church must take into consideration the primary mission of the kingdom: to grow, expand, and advance, while attacking and diminishing the kingdom of evil.

Jesus said His kingdom is like a grain of mustard seed, which grows into a tree large enough for birds to nest in (Matthew 13:31, 32). He said it is also like leaven, which is hidden in three measures of meal until the whole is leavened (Matthew 13:33). Our King envisioned His kingdom growing. Until His day, the kingdom had essentially been limited to one nation, but He foresaw a different future. "This gospel of the kingdom shall be preached in all the world for a witness unto all nations; and then shall the end come" (Matthew 24:14). Jesus expected His kingdom to expand.

Our world is the kingdom of Satan, and the purpose of God's kingdom is to invade and overpower this realm of darkness. Local churches, serving as tangible expressions of the kingdom's presence, are vital outposts in this enterprise. As embassies in a foreign land, with their members as God's ambassadors, they exist to help fulfill the kingdom's mission.

This means missions/evangelism—the practical expression of the kingdom's chief mission—is the essential purpose of the church. Thus, we should list, not purposes (plural) of the church, but rather functions of the church, those activities which help accomplish the church's one purpose, its overarching mission.

When making a list prioritizing the functions of the church, missions/evangelism should not be included. To put it on this kind of list is to lose it in the middle of a muddle. Even if missions/evangelism is listed as the church's number one priority, a temptation remains to rationalize it away by saying, *Though we may not be doing well with number one, we are doing so well with numbers two and three that we are making up for our weakness in number one.* I understand this rationalizing process. I have practiced it for years.

When listed with other objectives, missions/evangelism tends to get lost in the shuffle. The surest way to keep missions/evangelism in its proper place is to set it apart as the church's purpose in helping fulfill the kingdom's mission, and then to list separately those functions of the church which support this one purpose.

To see the significance of this interpretation, let's return to my seminary discussion. Let's say the purposes of the church are missions/evangelism, worship, fellowship, ministry, and discipleship. Notice, missions/evangelism tops the list. This places it as the number one priority, but it is in this context often improperly viewed as separate and distinct from the other church functions. Let me explain.

In this scenario, worship can have its own reason for being, totally separate from missions/evangelism. We can corporately gather to praise and promote the King, but our worship does not necessarily have to be tied to the mission of the kingdom. Many churches which do a wonderful job of corporate worship do very little outreach.

The same problem can develop in the area of fellowship. If it is merely another item on our list, it can take on a life of its own, having as its purpose to make us feel good about one another, to encourage each other, to form for ourselves a spiritual support group. All this can be done without any reference to outreach. In fact, the friendliest churches are often the unfriendliest. Churches that take great pride in their fellowship are often the very ones so closely knit they are in essence a clique. Outsiders cannot break in. The friendliness of the believers with each other makes the left-out newcomers feel even more ostracized.

Also, ministry can stand on its own, slipping into a social service, never winning anyone to Jesus. It can become merely a way of believers helping one another in trouble. Even when done by believers for unbelievers, it can be done for its own sake, without any effort to win the one helped to Jesus. What begins as an attempt to offer a cup of cold water in Jesus' name easily degenerates into merely offering a cup of cold water.

Discipleship, if set in a list with missions/evangelism, can also justify its own existence in isolation. In my younger years, I once asked the evangelist Hyman Appelman what he deemed the greatest danger facing the church. I assumed he would say liberalism, but he instead replied, "The deeper life movement, for it will cause us to turn our focus inward on ourselves." Sad, but true. Many of our people take years of training in discipleship, in the deeper walk with Christ, yet never lead anyone to the Lord.

As you can see, missions/evangelism, even if number one on our list of purposes, can be crowded out by other items on the list. This will not be the case, though, if instead of missions/evangelism being number one on the list, it is elevated to its rightful role as the mission of the kingdom. When this is the case, the remaining items on the list have to be viewed and understood in light of their role in supporting the kingdom's mission. This scenario changes everything.

Worship will still function to praise and promote the King, but it will always seek to lead the worshiper to a specific response for missions/evangelism. The final objective of worship becomes, not adoration or contemplation in isolation, but a desire to further the cause of the King who has been exalted. He is deemed worthy of being worshiped by all peoples everywhere. It is interesting to note that the most used worship passage in the Bible ends with Isaiah saying, "Here am I, send me" (Isaiah 6:8).

This interpretation of corporate worship certainly adds more meaning to the offering time in our worship services. It is not merely a time of giving our money, but a time of saying we offer our money to demonstrate our desire and intent to give ourselves in service to our King and the mission of His kingdom.

There has been a movement among pastors and leaders that should remind us to view worship in the context of evangelism. Even if we cannot lead our churches to become more seeker-oriented, all of us should at least move toward the position of being seeker-hospitable. Strange and archaic words can be removed from our worship. We should use words unbelievers can understand. For instance, say lesson instead of sermon, prayer instead of invocation or benediction, non-Christian instead of unregenerate.

Modern instrumentation can be added to our music. This does not detract one whit from our own people's enjoyment and involvement in worship, yet enables non-Christians not to feel too terribly out of place.

In this new scenario, the purpose of fellowship is activity the world can see to experience one of the main benefits of kingdom citizenship. Jesus said, "By this shall all men know that ye are my disciples, if ye have love one to another" (John 13:35), but the lost can only see our love for each other if they are invited to spend time with us. Cornelius invited others to join him. The Samaritan woman also brought others. The Bible says, "God sets the solitary in families" (Psalm 68:6). The lost need to see first hand in the local church how God can use it to become a community for the lonely, a belonging group for the hurting. Churches that have basketball and softball teams that requires each roster to include non-Christians illustrate using fellowship with a kingdom mission view.

The purpose of ministry, when viewed as complementary to missions/evangelism, is to woo people into the kingdom by showing them the kindness of our King. Steve Sjogren of Vineyard Church in Cincinnati, Ohio encourages his congregation to show kindness to people they encounter every day. Once they have completed their random acts of kindness, they leave a card inviting people to their church. Charles Roesel of First Baptist Church in Leesburg, Florida promotes the concept of servant evangelism. His congregation performs acts of ministry to earn the trust to share Christ. This church has an enormously successful ministry to single mothers in their area. These are just two examples that show how acts of kindness and servant-styled ministry can be powerful tools for kingdom expansion.

This is not to say we neglect ministering to our own. We show compassion for our hurting members, we bind up our walking wounded and enable them to return to the forefront of kingdom warfare, where they find their greatest sense of purpose and personal fulfillment.

The purpose of discipleship in a kingdom mission setting is to promote behavior worthy of kingdom citizenship. A local church must teach its members how to obey (Matthew 28:19, 20), for only in this way can they become great in the kingdom of God (Matthew 5:19). In discipleship we train people how to grow in grace, share their faith, support missions, plant churches, translate the Bible, etc. In other words, we teach our members how to live effective lives, including how to spread the kingdom. *MasterLife*, written by Avery Willis (Nashville: Broadman & Holman, 1998), is an excellent example of how discipleship in personal growth can be dovetailed with an emphasis on outreach.

When missions/evangelism is held high, lifted to its rightful place as the kingdom mission, it does not get lost in the middle of a muddle. We need this kind of emphasis on outreach. Since at least three-fourths of the world's population is lost, how can we have any priority higher than advancing the kingdom? With regard to these unbelievers, we believers must realize their destiny, not ours, is the issue. It is not right for four billion people not to be bowing at Jesus' feet. He deserves the reward for His suffering.

Five times our Lord gave the Great Commission. "Go ye therefore, and teach [literally, make disciples of] all nations" (Matthew 28:19). "Go ye into all the world, and preach the gospel to every creature" (Mark 16:15). "Repentance for forgiveness of sin should be proclaimed in His name to all the nations, beginning from Jerusalem" (Luke 24:47 NAS). "As my Father hath sent me, even so send I you" (John 20:21). "Ye shall be witnesses unto me both in Jerusalem, and in all Judaea, and in Samaria, and unto the uttermost part of the earth" (Acts 1:8). Jesus was serious about His followers extending the borders of His kingdom.

For our churches to understand their role aright, missions/evangelism must become not what we do, but who we are. Every activity must in some way be tied back into the kingdom mission. We must discern what God is up to, and get in on what He is doing. We catch the wave He is on when we hear deep in our hearts, "This gospel of the kingdom shall be preached in all the world for a witness unto all nations; and then shall the end come" (Matthew 24:14).

CONSIDER THIS...

On a scale of one to ten, where would you rank your current missions enthusiasm?   1   2   3   4   5   6   7   8   9   10

Why this ranking?

How are you personally involved in missions?

What would you need to do to increase your missions activity?

In your opinion, what are the purposes of the church?

Do you believe any of these purposes is more important than any other? Why?

Read Matthew 24:14. Is something yet to be done by us to hasten the return of Jesus? Is our failure to spread the kingdom delaying His return? Explain.

Read Matthew 10:7. When we say "the kingdom of heaven is at hand," what do we mean? How would our hearers interpret this phrase?

CHAPTER 2

PAUL AND US

"I WENT ABOUT PREACHING THE KINGDOM."

– **Acts 20:25b** (NAS)

PRIORITIZING the mission of God's kingdom was the hallmark of Paul's ministry. Missions/evangelism was his heartbeat.

Paul the apostle, the great champion of the Gentile cause, gave himself to spreading the kingdom above all other public activities. We easily forget this truth. For as he extended his efforts more and more into the Gentile world, he less and less described Jesus as King, preferring to use the term *Lord*—the title reserved for Caesar, the king of the world in Paul's day.

Lest our response be "ho hum" to the apostle's fervor for prioritizing the kingdom mission, let's remember we Gentiles attend church today primarily due to his undaunted resolve. His zest for extending the kingdom of God and his bulldog determination to go boldly where no believer had gone before brought the gospel to our ancestors.

Christianity was born in the East, in Asia. Our Master, His disciples, and every Bible writer were Asian. Paul's first missionary journey was limited to Asia, but on his second journey, while crossing the western provinces of Asia, he was "forbidden of the Holy Ghost to preach the word in Asia" (Acts 16:6b). Paul decided God wanted him to go north toward another Asian province, but "the Spirit of Jesus did not permit" (Acts 16:7 NAS) him. Thus Paul kept walking his original westward direction till he ran out of west-bound roads at the west coast of Asia. He arrived at the city of Troas, seeking God's will about what to do and where to go next.

This Asian man, serving an Asian Master and carrying an Asian message and sitting in an Asian city, heard his God in essence say, "Take My kingdom to Europe." "A vision appeared to Paul in the night: a certain man of Macedonia was standing and appealing to him, and saying, 'Come over to Macedonia and help us.' And when he had seen the vision, immediately we sought to go into Macedonia, concluding that God had called us to preach the gospel to them" (Acts 16:9, 10 NAS).

Putting out to sea from Troas, Paul "ran a straight course to Samothrace" (Acts 16:11 NAS), the island from which the Greek god Poseidon was said to have surveyed the plains of Troy. Homer called Samothrace "Poseidon's island." Be assured, had Poseidon seen the invasion of Paul approaching, his memories of the Trojan War would have dribbled into insignificance. He would have screamed an alert to his comrades on Mt. Olympus, "We are doomed, the kingdom of the living God is coming toward us."

Across Europe's mythical deity network, news would have spread to the gods of the German forests, "We are doomed, the invasion from God's kingdom has begun." In Gaul (present day France) the gods would have deemed their country's recent conquest by Julius Caesar mere child's play compared to the new onslaught headed their way. The nature gods of the priestly Druids and the Celts would have fallen to their knees in horror, knowing their days of human sacrifice were numbered.

Via the Mayflower and ships of the Puritans, God's kingdom invaded our shores. Now we find ourselves caught up in this larger-than-life drama. God's kingdom continues to call for advancement. Missions/evangelism remains this world's greatest need.

Many believe the time has come for a pivotal shift in the direction of the kingdom's advance. Some feel it is now time for us Westerners to try to launch a spiritual counter-attack, to seek to return the kingdom of God to its Eastern roots. Over the last two millennia, the gospel has had its greatest impact in the West. Maybe the time has come for us to return the favor by launching an all out spiritual assault on the homeland of our faith.

Many futurists are speculating that the third millennium of Christianity will belong to Asia. No one can be sure of this, but one truth is certain. God demands that we extend His kingdom, and Asia needs it badly, for the saving of souls from hell, for the enacting of human rights, for the lifting of women and children to higher dignity, for the helping of the poor, for the increasing of benevolent institutions, and for the honoring of Jesus. He deserves to be bowed before by the teeming masses of Asia.

Do not misunderstand. No one is saying "Asia only." The kingdom of God not only beckons us to never-reached frontiers; it also calls us to regions already touched. God's kingdom has infiltrated the Western World, but not penetrated every Western heart. Thus, even as we strive to extend His kingdom's geographical boundaries, we must seek to strengthen it in places already exposed to it. Pockets of resistance remain everywhere. This is why Jesus' command to go to Jerusalem, Judea, and Samaria is always as needful and relevant as the call to go to earth's uttermost parts.

The kingdom motto is ever, "To the ends of the earth, beginning next door." Thus, in addition to going to the other side of the world, we should adopt the streets nearest our church to prayerwalk, and establish relationships with our next-door neighbors to try to reach them.

Missions/evangelism is a dualistic approach. Both sides of the same coin must be emphasized. John Dowdy, Director of the Missions/Evangelism Division of the Missouri Baptist Convention, rightly said, "We need for the people in our churches to see a harvest, not just somewhere else and not just in their own field, but everywhere."

Now that we have an understanding of where missions/evangelism belongs in the church, let us now look at Christian history to determine how we came to be where we are now.

Any time an effort is made to determine the most important people in any field, the door is opened to error and disagreement. However, in the area of missions, four men certainly stand out as pillars, as inaugurators of new eras. In revisiting these men briefly, we may begin to better understand my generation's approach to missions.

William Carey, though certainly not the first missionary, is credited as being the father of the modern missions movement. The Moravian Brethren and a few other groups were sending out missionaries before Carey, but his life seemed to open the floodgate. He built a network back home that not only supported him, but became a pipeline of information and inspiration, helping others to begin to enlist in the mission enterprise. His work resulted in a flurry of missions boards and agencies, which spawned activity that most often followed trade routes established by the spread of the British Empire.

James Hudson Taylor brought a new dimension to the mission enterprise by fostering the "inland" movement. Pressing past where English-speaking merchants and traders had reached, he became in essence the grandfather of the modern unreached peoples movement, which is now sweeping churches and missions agencies in Europe and North America.

Cameron Townsend became convinced that people needed to hear the gospel in their heart language, not just in a trade language. He was asked by an Indian in Guatemala, "If your God is all-knowing, then why doesn't He know my language?" That question spurred Townsend to push for the Bible to be translated into every dialect and language on earth. His efforts resulted in the establishment of Wycliffe Bible Translators, and should earn Townsend acknowledgement as the father of our modern unreached peoples movement.

The fourth colossus of the modern missions movement was Donald McGavran for his contribution in the area of worldwide church growth. As the son of a missionary and a missionary himself, McGavran observed worldwide the dynamics which combine to make churches grow. From an internationally-educated mindset, he taught us what it takes to grow churches. He is rightfully called the father of the modern church growth movement.

I read McGavran's watershed book, *Understanding Church Growth.* It may be the greatest book, other than the Bible, I have ever read. I saw in it the genesis and formulation for the flood of books on church growth which have been written since. In reading the book, trying to find in it some clue for the lack of mission fire in many of my generation, I think I have begun to see what may have happened.

McGavran emphasized church growth within the context of each local church, and church growth through multiplication of the number of churches locally and all around the world. Note his three main theses: growth in each local church, increasing the number of churches locally, and increasing the number of churches globally through missions.

After McGavran, specialists continued to zero in on these three main emphases and to refine our understanding of each. Other pastors, scholars, leaders, and groups continued by marketing books on how to build a great local church, pushing for an increase in the number of local churches, and emphasizing the increase of churches globally through missions.

In the midst of this flurry of activity, many in my generation were making decisions regarding which direction we would go. What would be our main emphasis and where would we devote most of our effort?

Growing up in the tumultuous sixties, a time of moral and spiritual turbulence in the United States, we were affected by what we perceived to be the beginnings of an unravelling culture. We felt our country was falling apart. Overwhelmed by a sense of national and cultural urgency, we felt we had to save America. This being the case, I feel we made a generational choice, opting to give ourselves to evangelism and local church growth. We obviously did not abandon the missions enterprise. We promoted our special missions offerings, prayed for missionaries, and put our blessing on the missions effort, but our hearts were more wrapped up in saving a disintegrating culture. Intent on saving our own backyard, we found it hard to look intently overseas.

Now something new may be beginning to happen to my generation. Many of us are in some ways decreasing our efforts to save America. Do not misunderstand. We love that country and would die for her, but we are beginning to realize, if she is to be saved, God will have to intervene with an awakening. Our efforts to bring about political or social solutions have not and will not suffice.

This is not to imply churches should abandon their role in the culture. We still need to urge our people to vote and continue as salt, light, and leaven in a lost and dying world. However, we need to take our national-cultural-Christendom agenda off the front burner. It is an important piece of the pie, but still only one piece and must not be allowed to consume us to the exclusion of all else.

This realization was part of what began happening to me a few years ago. I had given myself to 30 years of reading and learning all I could about local church growth and evangelism. I would have been offended if anyone had accused me of not being vitally interested in missions, but I was devoting precious little time and energy to the missions enterprise. I was not preaching many sermons on it, not spending much time in prayer about it, not going on mission trips, and not encouraging my people to personalize their own mission involvement. Thus, when God began to put a missions burden on my heart, I truly felt I was in the bleachers, watching the Great Commission being played out on a field far, far away.

CONSIDER THIS...

Where would you be today had it not been for Paul's missions/evangelism zeal?

Others brought the kingdom to our nation. What nations are you personally involved in taking it to?

Do you ever think of Asia's needs for the gospel?

Read Acts 16:6. Why would the Holy Ghost ever forbid anyone to carry His message to a particular place?

Read Acts 16:9, 10. If the Lord does not open a door to one location, then what do we do next?

THROUGH THE EYES OF **GOD**

CHAPTER 3

THE BANNER OF JESUS

"THE FORMER TREATISE HAVE I MADE, O THEOPHILUS, OF ALL THAT JESUS BEGAN BOTH TO DO AND TEACH."

– Acts 1:1

LUKE, the beloved physician, wrote Acts. His "former treatise" was the New Testament book which bears his name.

The gospel of Luke is a biography of Christ, telling us what Jesus "began both to do and teach." The book of Acts is a sequel, telling us what Jesus continues to do and teach through His people. Jesus is still at work. The gospel of Luke describes His ministry performed bodily on earth; Acts speaks of His ministry performed spiritually from heaven.

Everything believers do should be Jesus' work. We merely continue what He begins. There is no place in kingdom advance for self-glory. We must lose sight of ourselves, promoting not our name, but the name of Jesus. Jesus is in heaven representing us. We are to be on earth representing Jesus. The banner we march under bears only the name of Jesus.

Dr. William Newell once said to the head of the China Inland Mission, "Oh, do pray for me that I shall be nothing!" The director kindly said, "Newell, you are nothing. Take it by faith." We must ever come to the end of ourselves. Jesus is everything, we are nothing. John the Baptist said it well, "He must increase, but I must decrease" (John 3:30).

Our burning passion should be for the world to see Jesus in us, for whenever the world gets a taste of Him, glorious things happen. The two who walked with Him to Emmaus said, "Did not our heart burn within us?" (Luke 24:32). The same burning can still touch people's hearts.

JESUS "COMMANDED THEM THAT THEY SHOULD NOT DEPART FROM JERUSALEM." (ACTS 1:4B)

Preceding implementation of the strategy, Jesus told His disciples to stay together. Had Jesus not given them this command, they would have scattered immediately. Peter would have become disgruntled with the other 10 and said, "I go a fishing." James and John would have gone back to their boisterous "sons of thunder" lifestyle. Matthew would have remembered his good salary and returned to his tax desk. Simon the Zealot would have ended his "nice-guy" routine and gone after Matthew.

The disciples would have gone their separate ways, but Jesus knew they needed to begin together to be strong. Unfortunately, we often think we are spiritually stronger than we really are. We crave independence, but actually need each other. None of us can stand alone. While alone, Thomas doubted and John the Baptist wavered. When away from the others, Peter denied.

Paul, for good reason, went everywhere starting churches. He was creating togetherness-groups, safety nets. We cannot succeed alone. We need each other. To succeed, we need a close-knit base of operations. No one can do it alone. We have to work together. I have a preacher-friend who once went to the St. Louis airport to watch planes take off. He said he wanted to see something moving he was not pushing. A world view cannot be solely a pastor's plan, but has to be God's plan shared jointly by all in a local church. *Together* is the operative word in an effective world view.

"WHEN THEY THEREFORE WERE COME TOGETHER, THEY ASKED OF HIM, SAYING, LORD, WILT THOU AT THIS TIME RESTORE AGAIN THE KINGDOM OF ISRAEL?" (ACTS 1:6)

Jesus had been with His disciples three years, yet they did not understand the nature of His kingdom. They still expected Him to establish a political kingdom. Though their theology was off, we must give them credit for having total confidence in Jesus' ability.

The disciples deemed Jesus as absolute Lord, capable of anything. Though wrong in some of their details, they were right in having big dreams and huge plans, and expecting Jesus to do something God-sized. They had not always been this daring.

When Jesus died, they lost their confidence, but His resurrection from the dead changed everything for them forever. They now believed Jesus was capable of anything.

Their theology was terrible, but their sights were high. Though we may have better theology than the disciples did at this particular moment, where are our sights? They spoke of power; we speak of weakness. They spoke of the world; we speak of our community. They spoke of an empire; we speak of buildings. They longed to see things happen that were so unbelievable all would have to say they were of God. Much of what our churches do today could be done if God were non-existent. We need dreamers who will attempt things so remarkable that if they are accomplished all glory will go to God. We need to resurrect the spirit of William Carey, "Attempt great things for God; expect great things from God."

Something was astir in the disciples. A dream had captured their imaginations, a passion was burning in their hearts. Before a world view can be enacted as a church's program, it must be a dream in people's imaginations and a passion in their hearts.

When the desire to tell all the world about Jesus becomes a church's obsession, nothing in the world will be able to contain it. Jeremiah, due to rejection, tried to quit speaking for God, but could not, for it was like a fire shut up in his bones.

Brownlow North was driven by passion. He preached like one who had just escaped from a burning city, his ear still stinging with the yell of the dying and the roar of the flame, his heart grateful for his own wonderful escape. We, too, should share the gospel because we have a passion for lost and dying souls. Knox prayed, "Give me Scotland or I die." Henry Martyn landed on the shores of India and cried, "Here let me burn out for God." Young Mary Reed came home from India due to a sickness later diagnosed as leprosy. She sat down to die, but remembered a colony of 500 hopeless, repulsive lepers she had seen in India. She returned and spent 52 years with them. Even after she was healed, she stayed.

A world view will entail sacrifice similar to Jesus,' and thus require more than just a surface commitment. A Holy Spirit-generated intensity will be essential. A God-given dream will beckon us on, a God-given inner passion will propel us forward. Ask Jesus to keep a compass in our hearts and a globe in our view.

CONSIDER THIS...

Where do you see Jesus at work in your life, your church, your community?

Do you have a passion for the world to see Jesus in you and in your church?

What are you and your closest believing friends doing collectively to extend the kingdom?

What has your church done lately in advancing the kingdom that elicited an absolute sense of awe, causing people to say, "Only God could have done this?

Are you ready to sacrifice, to make more than a surface commitment to missions/evangelism?

What have you recently sacrificed personally to help someone else become a Christ-follower?

Read Acts 1:1-4. Should missions be done haphazardly, or should we seek God's guidance every step of the way?

Read Acts 1:6. The disciples viewed God's kingdom as political. Do we? We rightly seek to influence our culture, but do we sometimes expect things from politics that can only come through the spiritual?

CHAPTER 4

THE POWER SOURCE

"BUT YE SHALL RECEIVE POWER AFTER THAT THE HOLY GHOST IS COME UPON YOU AND YE SHALL BE WITNESSES UNTO ME."

– Acts 1:8

PEOPLE'S LAST WORDS have always been a cherished possession. John Wesley said near his death, "The best of all is, God is with us." Thomas Paine, famous revolutionary and bitter atheist, died saying, "My God, My God, why hast thou forsaken me?" The last words spoken by 21-year-old Nathan Hale still thrill us, "I only regret that I have but one life to lose for my country." Queen Elizabeth I died, lamenting, "All my kingdom for a few moments of time."

Jesus' last words to His disciples have always been especially precious to believers (Matthew 28:19, 20). They continue to be vital in understanding His intended strategy for kingdom advance.

"BUT YE SHALL RECEIVE" (ACTS 1:8A)

Jesus said His disciples would *receive* power, not generate it. The kingdom of Christ allows no place for self-dependence. The power to witness and do missions is not manufactured from within, but received as a gift from without.

Missions/evangelism requires strength beyond ourselves. It is power extraordinary. The power to reach the lost is a unique, distinctive force that must be earnestly sought of God in prayer. There are no shortcuts. Each individual must do his or her own persistent praying, seeking power solely from above. We talk about getting up a revival, but we might as well talk about getting up a thunderstorm. Revivals come down, not up. Heaven is in perpetual revival and we must pray for it to spill out onto us.

"POWER" (ACTS 1:8B)

Jesus spoke here of real power, an empowering of God that is explosive and changes everything in its wake. This anointing never leaves people in a sad, dreary, or monotonous condition. When heaven's energy falls, everyone knows it.

A woman kept telling D. L. Moody, "You don't seem to have power in your preaching." He asked her and others to meet with him every Friday at 4:00 p.m. for prayer. Not long thereafter, while walking a street in New York City, he felt an overwhelming power coming upon him. He rushed to his motel room and cried, "Oh, my God, stay thy hand." Moody rarely preached another sermon without someone being saved, and for years witnessed to at least one non-Christian daily.

Do not misunderstand. We are not speaking of a once-for-all-time experience, but rather of an event which sets in motion an ongoing process. Having an experience is no guarantee of keeping its results indefinitely. God never wants His power taken for granted. Even Moody had to admit, "I am a leaky vessel, and I need to keep under the tap." We must remain near the Source for the flow to continue, but while the power is flowing, it is impossible to contain.

The power of God energizes us for His work. When we are tired, the power sustains us. We do not have to be in the best physical condition to work for God. Through the valley, the power can uphold us. We do not always need a bundle of excitement to keep us going. When discouraged, the power can motivate us. When everything else inside us says quit, the power can enable us to hold on.

We need this invigorating power to stir our people. Many of our churches suffer from the mundane. Locked on the dead center once occupied by the disciples between the resurrection and Pentecost, their attitude is, "Whoever happens to enter the upper room can join us." We need God's impelling power to drive us out of our comfort zones into the combat zone.

The church is often like an army sitting despondently before a granite fort. We want to attack, but lack motivation and know-how. We are discouraged because we have no explosive power. Our cannon balls, when thrown by ourselves, can do no damage to the wall. We ram our cannon against the wall, but to no avail. Powder thrown against the wall has only made it ugly, not weak. We have cannon balls, cannons, and powder, yet all the while the enemy is perched on the wall laughing. But wait! What have we found? A match. No one on the wall is laughing now. The fort is ruined. All we needed was fire to make an explosion.

Churches have machinery to attack Satan. We need the spark. We hurl sermons at him, ram him with Bible studies, and powder him with insults. He laughs on the wall until he sees the spark. When fire from God falls on our machinery, the same sermons, Bible studies, and taunts drive Satan back to his hellish home.

"AFTER THAT THE HOLY GHOST IS COME UPON YOU" (ACTS 1:8C)

The Holy Spirit, mentioned over 40 times in Acts 1–13, became the dominant figure of the early church. No major decision was made, no significant step taken, and no important course embarked upon, without guidance from the Holy Spirit. Once His will and power were manifest, the people pressed ahead, expecting powerful things to happen. They believed it was better to look for Him everywhere than nowhere.

Spreading the gospel and being filled with the Holy Spirit are often placed together in Acts. Never try to separate them. We need a dread Champion to lead the charge against our dread enemy. Remember that we should expect resistance when advancing the kingdom. Spiritual warfare is especially intensified when we try to penetrate new cultures. Testing our commitment to the Lord is Satan's God-allowed job.

Satan hits weak spots in our armor. He will use our own personal ambitions against us, and play on our natural insecurities. The devil does not play by the rules; he hits below the belt. Satan will even stoop to attacking us through weaker persons we love around us. Plan to see victims. War always entails carnage. Our only hope is to be filled with the Holy Spirit, to have Him fight our battles for us, and to encourage everyone near us to stay steadfast in the spiritual disciplines such as daily Bible study and prayer time, regular worship attendance, etc.

"AND YE SHALL BE WITNESSES UNTO ME" (ACTS 1:8D)

Our assignment is clear—be witnesses. Bear testimony to what the Lord has done in and for us. Eloquence and finesse are not essential, nor is the power of logic of utmost importance. Winning arguments rarely wins souls. Few people are ever argued into the kingdom. If we are harsh and ugly in our presentation, the non-Christian may be subdued, but not won. We may put them in their place, but they are still headed for hell.

When rebuked by the council, Peter and John replied, "We cannot but speak the things which we have seen and heard" (Acts 4:20). We are not required to relate things unknown by experience. We are able to testify of the things of God because we are witnesses to the resurrection of Jesus through the new birth. We are unable to explain everything, but we can say, "This happened to me."

CONSIDER THIS...

How much time have you recently spent praying for God to anoint your missions/evangelism efforts?

Do people in your community talk about how powerful God's presence seems to be in your church? What do they say?

Which word would they be more likely to use to describe your church: miraculous or mundane? Why?

Are we faithful in missions/evangelism all the time or only when "excited" about it?

Read Acts 1:8. Do we seem to have all the power God intends for us to have? Do we think the early church had more power than we do? If we received God's power in fullness, how would it manifest itself?

Read Acts 4:20. Would a primary evidence of the Holy Spirit's empowering include a willingness and ability to witness to the lost?

CHAPTER 5

THE WORLD ARENA

"BOTH IN JERUSALEM AND IN ALL JUDEA AND IN SAMARIA AND
UNTO THE UTTERMOST PARTS OF THE EARTH."

– Acts 1:8

KINGDOM WORK allows no place for cowards. Jesus told His disciples to stay in Jerusalem, otherwise, the disciples would have gone somewhere (anywhere!) else. Rulers, soldiers, and the crowd who killed Jesus were still there. The Eleven would have loved to wipe from their feet the dust of the city which crucified Jesus.

"BOTH IN JERUSALEM" (ACTS 1:8E)

The Eleven would have wanted to go home to nice, quiet Galilee, but they had become the followers of One who never backed down in the face of danger. Jesus had attacked Satan at his stronghold—death. The devil kept trying to sidetrack Jesus, but Jesus kept coming. His followers were expected to show the same fortitude. Regardless of the dangers, the Eleven were to stay in Jerusalem. They were to go where they could find the most need, not the most safety and ease.

We all need a good dose of courage. A friend and I were eating one night in a noisy restaurant. People all around us were taking God's name in vain. Suddenly, my friend said loudly, "I've heard God's name so much in here I feel like I'm in church." That put a hush over the crowd.

The disciples, courageous to the core, were not persecuted for being Christians as much as for being bold witnesses. They were sold out to God. Nothing was as important to them as pleasing Him. Jerusalem was a tough place to serve, but they did what Jesus told them to do. Soon their detractors were forced to cry out, "Ye have filled Jerusalem with your doctrine" (Acts 5:28). Refusing to be denied, they saturated their city with the message of Jesus. Tenacity was their theme. It is easy to tire of reaching out to others, to draw up into a shell and minister only to those who come to us, but our duty is to keep reaching and touching the world, beginning where we are, at home.

"AND IN ALL JUDEA" (ACTS 1:8F)

Jerusalem was tough, but at least had the advantage of being where the disciples were. Judea required movement, travel, and overcoming inertia. To reach Judea called for inconvenience, a change of plans, an altering of living arrangements. The disciples were willing to make the necessary sacrifices because they loved Jesus more than anything else in the world. He was the obsession of their lives.

Reaching people requires rearranging our priorities. One of the largest obstacles to a world view is the fanatic desire believers sometimes have for a comfortable lifestyle. Little worthwhile will be accomplished until time and money are given generously to God. We must learn to live within our means, and to give beyond our means. Prepare to be inconvenienced. Even now begin getting out of credit card debt and out of superfluous time-consuming activities.

"AND IN SAMARIA" (ACTS 1:8G)

Jews considered Samaritans their enemies, but Jesus set the example for His followers when He talked to, visited with, and converted the Samaritan woman at the well (John 4). Love your enemies includes a responsibility to witness to them.

This can be difficult. Imagine being the ones who carried the news of Saul's conversion to the believers at Damascus. When we said, "Saul has been struck down" we would have been cut off in mid-sentence with shouts of joy. Imagine the shock as we restored order and said, "No, you don't understand! God knocked him down, not to kill him, but to save him!" Ananias could not believe Saul had been converted, though the message was delivered by God Himself (Acts 9:13).

Peter had deemed Gentiles unclean. When the vision came about Cornelius (Acts 10), Peter resisted, uttering the ultimate oxymoron, "No, Lord." God Himself had to convince Peter this attitude was disallowed in the kingdom of Christ.

We Christians of today, for all our bravado about loving our enemies, are not doing as well as we should in carrying the gospel to them. We are often too much like Jonah, who was actually saddened by the conversion of his enemies, and was unhappy to be charged with this responsibility.

There were several other provinces near Judea. Jesus could have used any of them in this verse, but listed Samaria as a way of reminding us we have no right to skip over anyone as we seek to spread His kingdom.

"AND UNTO THE UTTERMOST PART OF THE EARTH." (ACTS 1:8H)

Since there is only one God, He has to be the God of all peoples. No group can stake an exclusive claim on Him. The gospel of Jesus Christ is for everyone.

This part of our Lord's commission began to be fulfilled in earnest by the Antioch church. The church at Jerusalem began reaching out to others due to persecution after the martyrdom of Stephen, but the saints at Antioch fulfilled the Great Commission in a spirit of prayer and beautiful submission to God (Acts 13:1, 2). The latter church, the home base for Paul's missionary enterprises, mattered because they had an outward view.

When Jesus said go to "the uttermost," He was stating the impossible dream. The task was geographically impossible—the whole world had not yet been discovered. The challenge was financially impossible—the early Christians were predominantly poor, with precious few resources to support missionaries.

The mandate was linguistically impossible—Greek predominated, but the world nevertheless was divided into hundreds of languages. The task was numerically impossible—120 believers versus the whole world.

Impossible, impossible, impossible! But the disciples had heard Jesus say, "With God all things are possible" (Matthew 19:26), and they had seen evidence of the statement's truthfulness in His resurrection. Therefore, they were willing to try the impossible. Jesus said do it, and they lived and died trying. They determined it was better to burn out than to rust out.

When I think of a local church undertaking this perspective, my initial response is, "Impossible." The task is geographically impossible—we still do not have freedom of access to every part of the world. The challenge is financially impossible—the cost of travel, mass media, Bible distribution, translation, and supporting missionaries is overwhelming. The mandate is linguistically impossible—hundreds of languages remain untouched by Christian witness. The task is numerically impossible—few of us versus multiplied thousands of them in our towns, millions in our country, and billions around the globe.

Can we communicate the gospel to every person in our home towns? Our first reaction is, "Of course not." Our second reaction must be, "We have to, we have no choice, we have our orders." We have a similar response to our Judea, Samaria, and uttermost part of the earth. "Cannot" has to be replaced with "must."

Fortunately, no local church has to do everything needing to be done. Other Christians and churches labor with us. We just have to find that part of the task God calls us to do. We do not run out and start doing things at random. This would lead to frustration and failure. We must saturate every plan and possibility with prayer, seeking to learn what God wants us to do, plus how, when, and where He wants us to do it.

OUR STORY

Knowing we must discover God's plan for our church, I decided to gather a group of church leaders to meet with me on a weekly basis to discuss the mission enterprise of our church. I had used lunch meetings in the past to discuss with key leaders such things as prayer ministries and more effective evangelism methods. I had also brought people into my office in small groups over lunch to discuss what they liked most and least about our church.

Expanding on this concept, our staff compiled a list of church members whose assignment would be to help determine the future direction of our church. This group of 100 met on Wednesday evenings for several months. In preparation for these meetings, I asked them to read Acts 1–13 over and over again. I hoped this would stimulate discussions about what a New Testament church should be like.

In the early stages of this group's meetings, someone stated an obvious truth we had somehow forgotten or overlooked somewhere along the way. We do not remember who voiced the insight, but it changed the dynamic of our group drastically. Someone said Acts 1–13 can be summarized in one verse, Acts

1:8b, where Jesus said, "Ye shall be witnesses unto me both in Jerusalem, and in all Judea, and in Samaria, and unto the uttermost part of the earth." I'm sure we all already knew this intellectually, but there is a difference between having hold of a truth and having a truth take hold of us.

Based on our rediscovery of this mandate from Acts 1:8b, we subdivided our group into four parts. We formed a Jerusalem group, which for us was the city where our church is located. We had a Judea group, which for us was our state. Our Samaria group laid out plans for the United States of America. The uttermost group set its sights on international mission possibilities. By targetting all four areas, our outreach focus would hopefully keep the missions/evangelism focus in proper equilibrium.

These four groups met individually for a while, and then began meeting collectively on occasions to compare notes, and ensure we were heading in the same direction. Our objective was to establish missions goals in each of these four geographical zones to be accomplished by our church in this generation, by a specified year. We then broke these goals down into measurable milestones to be achieved in five-year increments. This would give us a step-by-step plan to accomplish our long journey of rediscovering a proper kingdom focus.

While this group of 100, which we began calling our World Viewers, was meeting, I received a form letter from the Foreign (now International) Mission Board of the Southern Baptist Convention, asking churches to consider adopting an unreached people group. Approximately 2,200 unreached people groups remained in the world at that time. Some 187 of these had a population of a million or more. The Board was asking for 187 churches to lock arms with them in adopting these 187 groups. I brought the letter to a World Viewers meeting, read it aloud to the group, and asked if we should follow up on it. They looked at me like I had lost my mind, and said, "Isn't that what we have been praying about and meeting for? Of course we should respond."

I wrote the Board and expressed our interest in adopting one of the 187 unreached people groups. They responded with a letter giving us five groups to pray about and consider. We distributed information sketches on the five groups to our World Viewers and began to pray over which, if any, God would want us to adopt.

CONSIDER THIS...

Do you find it difficult to be a bold witness for Jesus? Why?

Do you think your city is a tough place to witness, maybe even harder than Jerusalem was for the disciples? Why?

How has your church filled your city with your doctrine (see Acts 5:28)?

Jesus left heaven to win us; have we left home to win anyone lately? When did you last share the gospel with a neighbor? Describe that encounter.

Read Acts 1:8. What is your Jerusalem, your Judea, your Samaria, your uttermost? Which of these is the hardest region to witness in? Does being in missions require packing a suitcase?

Read Matthew 19:26. Would it ever be possible for your church to be involved in mission globally, as well as locally, for Jesus? How?

CHAPTER 6

GO.

"FROM JERUSALEM, AND ROUND ABOUT UNTO ILLYRICUM,
I HAVE FULLY PREACHED THE GOSPEL OF CHRIST."

– Romans 15:19b

TO DO OUR evangelistic work, most of us need only a city street guide, but Paul fetched a compass and an atlas. He rode boats, walked Roman roads, and planted churches throughout the Mediterranean world.

When we remember the travel was much slower in Paul's day, the extent of his labors becomes incredible. Beginning in Jerusalem, his labors had, at the time of the writing of Romans, carried him through Palestine, Syria, Asia Minor, and into Europe.

He had stretched his ministry even to the most northwestern province of Greece—Illyricum, a region now included in Yugoslavia and Albania. Amazing! From Jerusalem to the very border of Italy itself—a distance covering well over a thousand miles. It is no exaggeration to say Paul was concerned about every soul in the world. Only time and logistics kept him from personally sharing the gospel with every person on earth.

In our day, due to advances in transportation and communication, the reaching of the whole world with the gospel is not a pipe dream or wishful thinking, but a mandate that could become reality if we can rekindle among us the fire and passion of Paul. If the church regained Paul's spirit, our world would soon be saturated with the gospel message.

"YEA, SO HAVE I STRIVED TO PREACH THE GOSPEL, NOT WHERE CHRIST WAS NAMED, LEST I SHOULD BUILD UPON ANOTHER MAN'S FOUNDATION." (ROMANS 15:20)

Paul wanted to take the gospel where it had never been taken before. He did not want to interfere in another man's harvest. Determined to be a pioneer, Paul felt he had to lead the way. A missionary passion blazed in his heart.

As a trail-blazer, Paul marked pathways, cleared new ground, broke up land, and planted the gospel in places where nothing but idolatry had reigned. Paul viewed every city a fortress of Satan, and saw himself as leading God's attack against it. From city to city, he barraged walls of evil. In every town demons saw him coming and cried out, "O no, Paul is coming. Satan, send reinforcements."

A danger in modern Christianity is a loss of Paul's pioneering spirit. It is easy to hide in our comfortable buildings. There is security within four walls. We are in danger of losing the spirit of daring that leads to the conquest of new fields, yet the world is still in need of Christians with Paul's drive.

Roads cry to be traveled. Sidewalks are eager to be walked. Doorbells long to be rung. Airplanes yearn to be ridden. The Internet beckons. The gospel pleads to be carried.

"WHENSOEVER I TAKE MY JOURNEY INTO SPAIN, I WILL COME TO YOU." (ROMANS 15:24A)

Paul had long desired to visit the Imperial City (Romans 15:23), and now thought he might be able to make a trip there. His work in the eastern Mediterranean world had been comprehensive. Believers and local churches were firmly established there and could carry out the further evangelization of those areas. This meant Paul was free to press on to new frontiers. His eyes were looking to the west.

Paul was coming to Rome, but his interest was not tourism. He intended for the Roman church to become the base for his western campaign, as Antioch had been for his eastern one. Still not fully satisfied with his missionary pursuits, Paul was planning a further extension of his work into faraway Spain.

Paul hoped to drive the gospel chariot all the way to the ocean. Spain was the westernmost limit of the known world. That fact alone would lure Paul to venture there. It would be natural for Paul to wish he could take the gospel message so far it could not be taken any farther.

Paul had a spiritual compulsion to travel on, to find more souls in darkness. As long as there was a road to travel, Paul was determined to follow it. This drive has been reproduced in every missionary, no matter how great. They are driven to share Jesus with those who need to hear.

When David Livingstone volunteered as a missionary, the London Missionary Society asked where he would like to go. "Anywhere," he replied, "so long as it is forward." Once he reached Africa, he kept pressing forward, going farther than any white man had ever gone before in that land. Haunted by the smoke of a thousand villages he could see in the distance, he felt compelled to carry the good news to people who had never heard it.

How we should weep when we contrast ourselves to such missionaries and the great apostle. Their motto was "Go, Go; farther, farther; onward, onward." We, however, rather than carrying the gospel to people, often act as if the gospel were a heavy load, too bulky to carry. We treat it like an exotic plant that has to be put in one spot and left there. We act as if the seed we are to sow is scarce. God gave us a sword with which to do battle, but rather than use it, we put it on display like a museum piece.

We chide people for not coming to our church buildings, but we need to chide ourselves for not leaving our buildings enough. God never told non-Christians, "Come to church." He rather told the church, "Go to non-Christians."

Interestingly, it is doubtful Paul ever made it to Spain. No early tradition links Paul with that country. His life plans were derailed by his arrest in Jerusalem, which led to his two-year imprisonment at Caesarea. From there he was taken in chains to Rome, where he was imprisoned for another two years. His prison letters indicate that by the time of his release, he had changed his mind and planned to go east rather than west.

Paul was not the last believer to have plans go awry. Like the rest of us, he had intentions and dreams that failed. Life is unpredictable. God alone knows the end from the beginning. Do not be afraid to make plans, but be sure not to idolize those plans. We are not to worship our dreams and ambitions. Remember, God is Lord over our plans. If our dreams turn to ashes, do not rebel. Instead, yield happily to God's sovereignty. Confess His right to do with us whatever He wants.

Many relate to the frustration of Paul. I once lost all my dreams, goals, and ambitions in one bundle. Every one of those dreams, goals, and ambitions could have been contained in a building of four walls, a city street guide, and a local church's organizational chart. Now, over a decade later, older and hopefully wiser, I have a new set of dreams, goals, and ambitions, which I share in common with a wonderful church that has been on its own spiritual pilgrimage for 120 years. Four walls, a city map, and our church's organizational chart are no longer for us the end, but the beginning. God has collectively given us grace to see that proclaiming the gospel to all the earth, as Jesus commanded, matters most.

I challenge us to take up the mantle of Paul, to help him continue his missionary journeys. Paul did not make it to Spain, but a later generation of believers made sure his epistle did. Other generations have also helped him be successful elsewhere. In over 1,000 different languages, Paul still travels to the corners of the globe with his message. How appropriate! The pioneer still presses on, and I urge us to help him continue.

What will prompt us to go and continue his efforts? The great motivator in life is neither will nor intellect, but rather desire. Thought knows what should be done, and will resolves to do, but desire gives power to accomplish.

Learn what a person desires, and you will know the direction his or her life is moving. We do what we want to do. St. Augustine the missionary confessed, "Whithersoever I am carried forward, it is desire that carries me." We, too, need a holy desire. Thus, I ask us to pray for a desire to win people everywhere, in our Jerusalem, our Judea, our Samaria, and all around the world. Pray for a burning compulsion for God's perspective. It alone will suffice, and God alone can provide it.

OUR STORY

So it was becoming with our World Viewers and myself. While we were waiting on the International Mission Board to respond to my letter about adopting a people group, we became aware of Global Focus. Global Focus was an organization which had entered a five-year contract with our International Mission Board to help churches turn from solely a local church growth mind-set to a world-wide kingdom outreach mind-set. Since this was exactly what we were trying to do, the World Viewers encouraged me to contact Dr. Larry Reesor, founder and president of Global Focus, to share with him the pilgrimage our church was beginning.

I asked our church's executive pastor, John Edie, to make the initial contact with Global Focus and bring us a report. Just before leaving town for a conference in Nashville, Tennessee, John called

Dr. Reesor's office. When he asked to speak with Larry, the secretary said he was out of town with his wife, who was attending a real estate meeting in Nashville. John mentioned he was heading to Nashville and wondered if the secretary could tell him the motel where Larry was staying in case the two might get together for breakfast or lunch. The secretary named the motel—the same place John had reservations to stay in Nashville. This was just the beginning of amazing things that would happen to our church and its members because we were dealing in matters important to the heart of God Himself.

John met with Larry in Nashville, and brought back a report. We immediately realized our church and Global Focus were on the same page. Dr. Reesor added us to his schedule, literally squeezing us between two already-scheduled plane stops. He made a special trip to our city for the sole purpose of meeting with our group. His message resonated with our people. If we had any lingering reservations about pursuing with enthusiasm the worldwide missions/evangelism enterprise of God, the Holy Spirit used Larry to dispel them.

Larry encouraged us, saying we were already way ahead of the game by having organized our mission focus around the four geographic divisions presented in Acts 1:8. He told how God's kingdom is rapidly spreading all around the world, and spoke of the revival sweeping many countries. We were literally breathless by the end of the evening. God was up to something in our midst. Our group could feel a new breeze blowing in the sails of our ship of state. We sensed we were being caught up in a drama bigger than our own little worlds.

Do you want to see every soul on the planet saved?

Has your church considered taking the gospel where it has never gone before?

Do you have a passport? If you sensed God's call to go, how quickly could you respond?

When pondering your role in missions, does the phrase "farther and onward" ever come to mind? How does that phrase motivate you?

Have you invested money in helping Paul's writing be translated into a new language?

Read Romans 15:29. Paul traveled over 1,000 miles to share the gospel. How far should we be expected to go?

Read Romans 15:20. Does God still place value in taking the gospel to places it has never been heard before?

CHAPTER 7

LIVING IN DEBT

"I AM DEBTOR BOTH TO THE GREEKS, AND TO THE BARBARIANS;
BOTH TO THE WISE, AND TO THE UNWISE."

– Romans 15:14

PAUL serves as an example of one who had a burning inner compulsion for kingdom advance. He was impelled from within toward missions/evangelism.

"Greeks" referred to all who spoke the rich Greek language; "Barbarians" referred to those whose speech was foreign. "Greek and Barbarian" was a way of saying all people of all languages, wherever they lived.

"Wise and unwise" means learned and unlearned, the cultured and the crude, the civilized and uncivilized. Paul sensed himself a debtor to all people, regardless of nationality or mental ability.

Surely if the world ever owed a man anything, it was to Paul. He gave his all for the betterment of humanity. Nevertheless, he said, "I am debtor." No soil is more fertile for productivity than the pressure of a great debt. Obligation is the mother of productivity.

The instant Paul was saved, he knew he was in debt to Jesus. And Jesus collects payment on this debt through the lost world. A major evidence of our gratitude to God is in trying to give others what has been given to us.

People are precious in God's sight. They have an inherent dignity which compels us to serve them. Of every person it can be said, "Here is one for whom Jesus died." Paul was keenly aware he had been entrusted with the only message that meets the need of lost humanity. The very fact he had it made him responsible for those who needed it. He owed a debt.

When Louis Pasteur discovered bacteria spread disease, he was immediately a debtor to the human race. He had to share the news. When Jonas Salk developed the polio vaccine, he was immediately a debtor to mankind. When Edward Jenner developed a safe smallpox vaccination, he was immediately under obligation.

The world needs healing, and believers have the only medicine to cure it. This fact alone is sufficient to prescribe duty. No excuse can vindicate a person who knows the secret of health, but keeps it from the sick.

During one of Britain's civil wars, a governor was convicted of treason against the king. Intercession was made on his behalf, and the king issued a pardon from the death sentence. Unfortunately, the pardon fell into the hands of the governor's bitter enemy, who kept it locked up until after the execution.

We feel horror-struck at the ruthlessness of a man who, having the pardon of a fellow man in his possession, could keep it back and let him die. However, could the Lord point His finger at many of us and make the same accusation?

The Lord has entrusted us with a pardon to spare people from everlasting death. The pardon is available to all, sent to all, designed for all, blood-bought for all; we must get this news to all.

A child of God who feels a debt to the lost will find a way to discharge the duty. The Christian who realizes "I am debtor" is the one who will be impelled to do the most and best work for Christ. A sense of obligation is the best root from which to grow genuine missions/evangelism. *God, give us a sense of debt.*

"SO, AS MUCH AS IN ME IS, I AM READY." (ROMANS 1:15A)

Paul not only confessed he was a debtor, but also admitted he was anxious to pay on the debt. "I am debtor" and "I am ready" are two confessions at the very heart of all true work for God. We owe people, and need to be about the task of paying on the debt by means of missions/evangelism.

The word *ready* comes from a word which means to be in a heat, as in running a race. It points to eagerness that breathes hard, panting heavily and rapidly. Desire was astir within Paul. He had a passion to preach in Rome.

"As much as in me is" is the key phrase. It reveals the extent to which Paul sensed his debt. The debt was more than he could pay in one lifetime. It required his whole self. He would pay on the debt until all his resources were exhausted in death. All he was and had would be applied to the debt.

Paul's life demonstrated the sincerity of his intentions. On the Damascus Road he asked, "What wilt Thou have me to do?" Immediately after his conversion, Paul preached Christ in the synagogues of Damascus and Jerusalem. God had to stop him and send him to Arabia to meditate and pray. After being stoned in Lystra, he returned in a few days to see how the Christians were doing. When he saw the vision of the man of Macedonia, he immediately endeavored to go there. Though the Jews at Jerusalem desired his death, he went there with an offering for the saints. Paul was impelled to do the kingdom's work.

David Brainerd, another man who sensed an inner urgency for missions/evangelism, died a horrible and slow death at age 29 due to tuberculosis. His clothes often dripped with sweat caused by his recurrent fever and chills. He was a missionary to the Native Americans and gave himself entirely to their service. Blood was often left on the snow where he had knelt in prayer for them. He preached to them as often as possible. As his strength continued to fail, he preached while seated. Often the Native Americans had to carry him home after the service. Finally, the Native Americans came to his house and he preached while lying down. When he was taken (in vain) to Massachusetts to recover, he wrote letters to them. When too weak to write, he dictated letters by whispering. When too weak to whisper, he prayed for them. May God grant us the spirit to say, "So, as much as in me is, I am ready." May He impel us to the task.

"TO PREACH THE GOSPEL TO YOU THAT ARE AT ROME ALSO." (ROMANS 1:15B)

By any human standards, Paul was crazy. His desire appears suicidal. Paul, utterly weak in himself, and tormented by a thorn in the flesh, was going to march into Rome and preach the gospel. He was going to proclaim Jesus' death, burial, and resurrection. Paul was going to preach in Rome that the true King of the world was a man who had been crucified by a Roman governor!

Paul wanted Rome. He was going to Caesar's town to tell men the real King was a Nazarene despised by Jews and crucified by Romans. Paul believed in going for the head when fighting with a serpent, and he knew that influence exerted in Rome would spread through the Empire.

Rome, at best, would be an icy atmosphere in which to share the gospel. We all live in the midst of a spiritual ice age, which tends to press upon us relentlessly. We can either let the ice bring down our temperature, or let it stimulate us to put more fuel on the fire and thereby melt the ice.

No one could have faulted Paul if he had been reluctant when confronting Rome. It was the hideous time of Nero. The city was a moral sewer. To shrink from going there would be normal, but Paul never batted an eye, remaining undaunted and fearless.

Where can we find greater bravery than Paul's? When he arrived at Rome, he himself was in chains, and preached to the Romans about a man they had already disposed of.

Alexander, Caesar, and Napoleon marched with armies to enforce their will upon men. Paul marched with Christ alone to the center of the world's might. He took the Word of God right into Satan's strongest trench.

Paul was ready to do all he possibly could to proclaim the message of Jesus the King to the city of kings. Paul's victory was sure because his weapon was sure. He knew the Word, sharper than any two-edged sword, would topple the armies of Satan. When the Knights of Germany offered their swords to Luther in behalf of his cause, he replied, "The Word shall do it." He was right.

Paul had a message of certainties. He had a word from God, and did not hesitate to say he had the last word regarding salvation. He preached an authoritative message with authority. The result was staggering. Within 10 generations after Paul's arrival, 1,750,000 Christians had been buried in the catacombs at Rome. By the year A.D. 250 one-fifth of Rome was Christian; by A.D. 313 Christians had received religious freedom; by A.D. 380 Christianity was the official religion of the Roman Empire. One man impacted Western civilization and turned the tide of history.

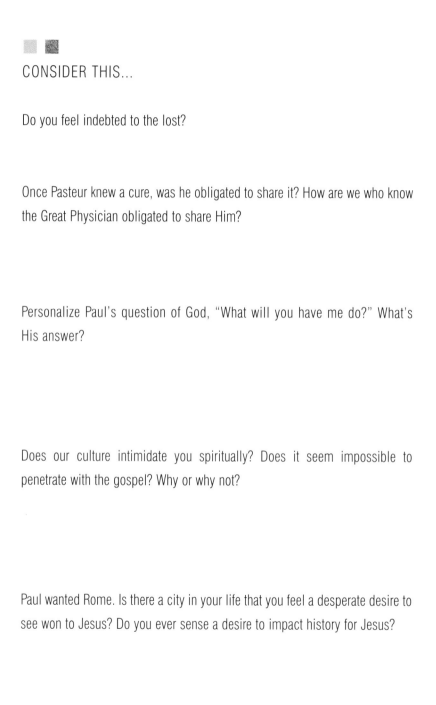

CONSIDER THIS...

Do you feel indebted to the lost?

Once Pasteur knew a cure, was he obligated to share it? How are we who know the Great Physician obligated to share Him?

Personalize Paul's question of God, "What will you have me do?" What's His answer?

Does our culture intimidate you spiritually? Does it seem impossible to penetrate with the gospel? Why or why not?

Paul wanted Rome. Is there a city in your life that you feel a desperate desire to see won to Jesus? Do you ever sense a desire to impact history for Jesus?

Read Romans 1:14, 15. How can you have as much conviction and determination as Paul displayed? In our world today, is there still a place for someone as driven as Paul was? Explain.

Read Acts 27:24. Jesus often said, "Fear not." Did He mean He would never put us in a witnessing situation that might make us feel uncomfortable? What did He mean?

CHAPTER 8

OUR STORY CONTINUES

"MY YEARS OF PASTORAL PRAYING HAD NEVER PREPARED ME FOR THIS.
I FELT I WAS A DWARF AMONG GIANTS."

THROUGH THE SUMMER of 1997 our church leadership campaigned to inform our people of the new mission enterprise our World Viewers were recommending. We did everything we knew to do: mass mailouts, bulletin inserts 13 Sundays in a row, sermons, special music, testimonies, video promotions, etc. These were all used to impact the hearts of our people.

The response of our people was initially slow and skeptical. I was a bit frustrated until one night, while in prayer, I suddenly realized I was responsible for any lukewarmness in the response of my people. Our church members had become what I had made them. The heart, passion, and zeal of my generation of preachers had focused primarily on local church growth. The people in the pews had become what the sermons had made them. We taught them well. It began to dawn on me that change would come—our people do love the Lord, His Word, His church, and His kingdom, they do want to do right—but the change would come gradually. Just as it had taken a process to begin changing me, it would take another process to change them. I would have to be an encourager and try to nudge them along, but the change itself would have to be implemented by God Himself.

Ultimately, the Lord alone can change people. God anoints our preaching and teaching. He empowers the message as it passes from the pastor's heart to his mouth and then on to the people. Only He can then anoint the hearing, and make the message go from the people's ears to their hearts.

At summer's end, our people voted to adopt our proposed World View Document (see Appendix). They agreed with it in principle, but the enthusiasm I longed for was not yet evident. They had voted with their hands. It would take awhile for them to vote with their hearts.

We began implementing procedures set forth in the World View Document. We prayed for effective leaders, and called four of our lay people as volunteer staff members. They were given office space, access to secretaries, and attended staff meetings. They were assigned oversight of our missions enterprise in our city (Jerusalem), our state (Judea), the USA (Samaria), and international work (uttermost). We arranged missions projects and trips for those who felt led to hands-on experience in mission work. We also began networking with members of our church who had direct connections with people on the mission field.

Before continuing, let me tell the end of the story about our effort to partner with the International Mission Board in adopting an unreached people group. As the World Viewers were praying over the five options the International Mission Board had sent us, one of our group told me he was feeling a strong sentiment for the Muato people (name fictitious to protect Christians there from harm). He was the only World Viewer to mention a specific group to me.

A few days later, on a Friday, I was in my office preparing Sunday's sermon. A friend I had not seen in over six years was driving by our church. Seeing my name on the church sign, he stopped to chat awhile. When I had last seen him, he was a pastor in the St. Louis area, but had since gone to work for the Missouri Baptist Children's Home.

My secretary stepped into my office to say a gentleman was out at the reception desk wanting to see me. I asked who it was. She replied, "Wayne Crull."

"Wayne Crull!" I said as I jumped from my seat and headed for the reception desk. Memories flooded in. Some 11 years earlier God had used Wayne Crull to help me overcome a long battle with depression. At a preachers' meeting, I had heard Wayne tell how God had delivered him from depression after years of dealing with baggage left over from his service in the Vietnam War. After hearing Wayne speak, I for the first time, thought maybe I could win over depression. I had long before decided it was just a natural part of my make-up. I dealt with it, but never really thought about actually overcoming it. Wayne was willing to meet with me privately, and referred me to a couple of good books. With help from God and my wife, I began to emerge from a deep blue funk.

When I moved to a pastorate in Arkansas, years and distance came between Wayne and me, but my sense of debt to him has never waned. I will owe Wayne Crull as long as I live. To spend a few minutes with him in my office on a Friday afternoon would be sheer joy. The instant we saw one another at the receptionist's desk, we hugged and started joking. It seemed we had never been apart.

We sat in my office and chatted about old times for awhile. When Wayne asked what was new in my life, I told him about the new missions enterprise we were involved in. He could sense my excitement. I told him I was especially excited about the possibility of our church adopting an unreached people group.

At that point Wayne mentioned he had a friend who was working with an unreached people group called the Muato. I could not believe what he had just said, and responded, "That's impossible, Wayne. There are over 2000 unreached people groups in the world. The International Mission Board has asked us to pray about five, and one of them is the Muato. It's not possible that you would walk in here and out of the blue mention them."

Wayne hesitated to reply, but finally asked, "Is it spelled M-u-a-t-o?"

I said, "Yes, but this still cannot be." I felt rising in me a level of excitement I had not experienced in God's work in a long time. If Wayne was correct, I knew we were in the middle of one of the biggest God-things in my life. I have a friend who often says, "It's not odd, it's God," but this seemed to be off the chart of believable possibility.

Wayne promised he would try to find the whereabouts of his friend the following Monday morning. From Friday afternoon until Monday morning, I was in an agitated state of hyper-excitement. I felt something miraculous was afoot, as if I had stepped into a God-dimension of massive proportions. All through the weekend I tried to keep my mind on other things for fear of being disappointed.

At 8:00 a.m. Monday, I telephoned Wayne's office. When he answered, I immediately asked, "Have you found her?" He laughed and said, "John, I just walked into my office. I promise I will try to find where she is and get back with you later today."

The hours crawled by. I knew a little bit about what Wayne was up against. Trying to find info on an undercover worker in a restricted access country is like trying to find a CIA agent. Finally, late Monday afternoon, Wayne called. He had found her. She was, in fact, working among the people of Muato. He had located a mutual friend who knew what church she had grown up in, and when he called that church, he was able to convince them he had worked with her on several occasions. They finally believed he could be trusted, especially since he already seemed to know what group she was working with.

When Wayne confirmed the people group, I knew immediately my life was inextricably connected with these people of whom I had never heard a few weeks earlier. In that moment, the people of Muato became *my* people, as much mine as the people God has given me to shepherd as pastor. It was a defining moment in my life, one I find difficult to describe adequately.

For security reasons we refer to our lady in the field as Mary. Wayne was able to give me the phone number of her aged father. I called him long distance and began to speak to him of his daughter. He was reluctant to talk about her to a stranger. As we continued to talk, we discovered we had been pastors at two small Southeast Missouri churches only about five miles apart. This gave us a spirit of camaraderie which seemed to set him at ease. Finally, he gave me Mary's overseas phone number.

Mary and I talked several minutes. In fact, it was a long and expensive phone call. A new world of opportunity was opening before me and I could not seem to get enough information. She happened to be heading home in a few days for one year of furlough in the United States. We ended our conversation, agreeing to talk again when she arrived home. I told her we would want to have her come and speak to our church about the people of Muato.

This sequence of events has been told and retold at our church in many different settings. It has become part of the fiber that makes our missions mosaic so wonderful. I think all of us who were among the World Viewers will always have a soft place in our hearts for the events of those formative days in our mission endeavor.

The World View Document was set in motion. Global Focus became our partner and we had new staff members working on missions. An unreached people group had become part of our lives. Everyone looked happy, and all seemed well. Then Larry Reesor, president of Global Focus, dropped a bombshell. "John, your church has adopted an unreached people group, and the International Mission Board really thinks all pastors who do this need to travel and see their adopted group firsthand."

I do not travel well, being the ultimate homebody. Ruth and I rarely ever spend a night apart. An overseas trip was out of the question. I adamantly refused, but Reesor was equally stubborn. He had already planned a trip to the very country where my adopted people were located. Several pastors and Jerry Rankin, president of our International Mission Board, were going. Larry insisted I go. I kept deferring, hoping John Edie, our church's executive pastor, could go in my place.

A few weeks later, John, Larry, and I were sitting in my office discussing the trip. Larry was talking as if I were going. When I reminded him I did not plan to go, he looked at John Edie, who quietly said, "Pastor, you *have* to go." I did not like the sound of that phrase. "What do you mean, I *have* to go?" John went on, "We have already written the check and cannot get our money back." The euphoria of my mission zeal suddenly waned. I felt a momentary hesitation, but somehow knew this was the right thing to do.

The next several weeks were difficult. I dreaded the upcoming trip. Having to take a battery of shots made things worse. Plowing through paperwork for passports, visas, and trip plans didn't help my outlook, nor did shopping and packing. The thought of leaving Ruth and my family saddened me. I asked my church people to pray for me, and they did.

After two domestic flights, I connected with Dr. Reesor and his group in a large coastal city here in the United States. Our flight across the ocean seemed to last forever. Reading Billy Graham's autobiography, *Just As I Am*, helped pass the long hours.

Once we arrived overseas in a safe coastal city, we were briefed on the security risks and potential dangers which were ahead. We were also introduced to the guides who would lead us into interior areas.

Since my connection with our unreached people group was in the United States on furlough, I was placed with another pastor, who was going in with his connection to see the group his church had adopted. His people group is closely kin to ours, and a trip to see them was deemed by the International Mission Board as sufficient for me to see what my group was like.

With two people I had never met, I headed into the interior of a country hostile to the good news. Major bonding took place over the next few days. I became fast friends with two people who shall forevermore be special in my heart.

As two Baptist pastors with a blond, female guide, we were stared at everywhere we went. I think people thought she was a high-ranking official, and we two guys were her bodyguards. The farther into the interior we went, the more our light-colored skin and her light-colored hair seemed to attract attention.

We rode airplanes, a big bus, a sleeper bus, and small buses. Reaching our final outpost required renting a taxi. The driver had a small jeep with no windows and carried his battery with him whenever he left the vehicle. Along the way I had to learn the intricacies of a "squatty potty," an interesting experience for any Westerner.

After days of travel, we reached the town from which we would make our final ascent to the village of my companion's adopted people group. The bus left soon after we arrived in town. There would be no more buses until morning.

Several young men began to gather closely around us and laugh at us. Fortunately, our guide knew the local language. This seemed to calm their exuberance a bit.

Carrying our luggage, we trekked two blocks uphill to the hotel where our guide had made reservations. At the front desk, she and the clerk began a heated exchange of words. The other pastor and I knew something was wrong. I remember his whispering, "We need to pray." Whatever the problem was, we knew we were trapped overnight in this town.

Local government officials, having learned we were coming, had forbidden the two hotels in town to accept us. They had canceled our reservations and were requiring us to stay overnight in the government guest house.

Our guide was visibly shaken. She had been working in this town for several months, hoping to secure a position at the local school for us to place there an English as a Second Language teacher. I think she knew at that very instant that all her efforts had been in vain. The locals had tantalized her, leading her to think they had a place for her, but once the government officials caught wind of it, they killed the project.

Though fearless as any person I have ever known, our guide was obviously taken aback by this turn of events. The three of us walked back out to the street, went another block uphill, turned left, and walked another two blocks uphill, still accompanied by the local young men who seemed pleased at our plight.

The government guest house was a gloomy, dilapidated, and disorderly slum of a place. As our guide negotiated with the desk clerk, who was determined to charge an exorbitant sum, I sat down on a couch in the lobby. As a huge cloud of dust (and critters, I think) enveloped my whole body, I immediately jumped up.

Once the negotiating ended, we were given two rooms. Our room was adjacent to the second floor lobby. Our guide was down the hall about 20 yards farther. We were given no keys to lock our doors. In fact, the doors had no locks. Our guide told us to put our things in our room and then to meet her downstairs again in the main lobby. She instructed us to say absolutely nothing out loud until we were back together again. The other pastor and I quietly put our things in the room, and silently returned to the lobby.

Once our guide arrived, the three of us silently walked down to the riverside in the middle of town. When we were way beyond earshot of anyone, our guide began to talk. Her words were spoken in barely a whisper. The tone of her voice told us all we needed to know. She had evidently been exposed. The local officials had probably learned what she was up to. Things did not look good. Facing a change in plans, we had to decide what to do next.

The original plan had been to spend two nights in town. We had intended on the first day to leave a gift for the local minorities museum, and ride up to see a village. The second day we had intended to spend at the school, seeking to court the favor of the administration there. I suggested we consider leaving town first thing in the morning, but the other pastor wanted to fulfill his mission. His church had sent him to see his adopted unreached people group. He felt he had to make it up to the village.

Our guide was also determined to press ahead with her plans. She wanted to give the museum a gift, and to talk with the school leaders.

By this time, night was falling. Our guide suggested we pray. We had to do this with our eyes open. While one of us at a time offered a whispered prayer, we kept watch to see if anyone was coming our way.

After prayer, we agreed on a plan. Rising early in the morning, and eating snacks we had brought with us, we would see if we could accomplish everything in time to catch the last bus out of town tomorrow evening.

Until then, the instructions from our guide were very simple: say nothing, the room was probably bugged. We returned to our quarters. Life had suddenly become very serious.

The other pastor and I went to our room and scooted a small end table in front of the door. We somehow felt this would at least slow someone down if they decided to break into our room. Not one word was spoken to each other, for fear we might be overheard saying something amiss.

My roommate took off his shirt and jeans and crawled into bed. I left all my clothes on. I had an unsettling feeling. I wanted to be prepared; I don't know for what, but I just wanted to be prepared.

A huge drinking party was going on in the government guest house. I was uncomfortable at the thought of being found out in a place filled with drunken officials. Their revelry continued unabated for hours.

At midnight all the noise abruptly stopped. In an instant everything became deathly silent. All I could surmise was that curfew had fallen. The remaining events of the evening continue to be an unnerving chapter in my memory.

After a while of silence, I heard loud steps coming closer and closer to our room. They stopped outside our door. A man began pounding on our door and barked out words in a language I did not understand. Within seconds I heard the footsteps leaving quickly and loudly.

Before long, I heard footsteps again. This time two men were coming. They were talking loudly, and the sounds of their steps seemed to be coming right to our room. Again, the steps stopped outside the door, and someone pounded on our door, yelling. All I knew to say was, "Who is it?" I yelled fairly loudly, hoping they would not sense any fear in my voice. The other pastor had jumped out of bed, trying to get his shirt and jeans on.

In the tense moments that followed, we heard the two men excitedly talking to each other. They then walked away.

As best we remember, the time was about 2:00 a.m. I spent the next four hours in unceasing prayer. I was never more scared. At the far end of our room, high on the wall, was an uncovered window I stared at the rest of the night. I don't know why, but for some reason I felt if we could make it till dawn, we would be okay. I had no logical reason to believe that, but did nonetheless. I still vividly remember when the first light of day began to appear in that window.

Once day broke, and we heard people milling around in the lobby, the other pastor decided he needed to check on our guide, as we had no way of knowing how she was. I stayed in the room while he quickly ran down the hall and knocked on her door. She was fine. No one had bothered her.

Since we were awake anyway, and had decided the night before that we would get an early start, we went ahead and dressed for the day. We went to the museum and left a gift for the proprietor. Then we went to the school and talked to several people in charge.

Our guide could tell things had changed because the attitude was not nearly as open as it had been.

It was disheartening to be in town when a kingdom worker found out her work there was finished. We were receiving intense training regarding some of the trials and troubles people can experience on a hostile field. I hope our presence helped to bring her a measure of comfort and strength.

We secured the jeep taxi driver, who installed his battery, and drove us up into the mountains to see a village. I remember the trip well. Tea fields stretched as far as the eye could see. A local travel agent who rode along sang for us love songs used in courtships by her people. I couldn't help but wonder if she were singing them more for our driver than for us.

My traveling partners were excited about this trip up the mountain. They wanted to see their adopted unreached people group up close. I was more excited about returning back down the mountain in time to catch the last bus out of town. My objective was crystal clear—get home safely and quickly.

As we approached the village, we disembarked the jeep, and walked the last several yards. I was glad I had now seen an unreached people group village, and had fulfilled all the International Mission Board expected of me.

Then another God-thing happened. As we began to see people of the village, I happened to turn and look at the other pastor. I think I was going to congratulate him on reaching his destination, but when I looked into his face, I saw the look of a pastor whose heart was inextricably connected with a people he had never seen before. I knew immediately I would return to see my own adopted people. The die was cast. I knew, up there on that mountain, that I would have to come back with my people group connection and visit a village of my adopted people.

Our trip down the mountain seemed less stressful. I guess once I decided to come back I was thinking, "Oh well, if they don't kill me this trip, they'll just get me next time." The fact I had decided to return seemed to relieve my tension. The travel agent asked us to sing a song. Our guide, obviously feeling she had nothing to lose in this area, started singing "Amazing Grace." We joined in with her. After the song, our guide gave the travel agent an English name, "Grace."

Later, in a large city so choked with smog that we could barely see or breathe, we observed the Lord's Day by ourselves in a motel room. To make sure we were not overheard, we sat close to one another and took turns whispering the letter of 1 Thessalonians, an applicable book when read in terms of unreached peoples. I couldn't help but think of my church back home, where the worship service would be loud and free. Worship in that motel room wasn't like worship back home, but was worship nonetheless.

Along the way, we met a few of our guide's associates, others who also secretly do what she is doing. My most vivid memory entails the way they prayed. Early in the trip, when one of them would say we should pray, we two pastors thought they meant we would stand in a circle, hold hands, sing "Kum Ba Yah," and then go to bed. Wrong! When these people pray, you have to clear your calendar.

They put their notes and books away, and find a place where they can sit comfortably for awhile. Then they begin to pray. Never had I heard prayers like these before. They cried out to

God for people groups I had never heard of. They claimed promises from Bible verses I had only casually read in the past. I remember one praying that God would loose the government's grip, reasoning that the Christians of their country had suffered so much persecution that they would now have the stamina to invade the Muslim countries with the gospel and be willing to die for it.

When it came my turn to pray aloud, I always felt very uncomfortable. My years of pastoral praying had never prepared me for this. I felt I was a dwarf among giants.

I had one more scare before arriving home. Several of our undercover people wanted someone to risk carrying letters home to friends and loved ones. I had done the best job of packing among those who went on the trip, and since I had the least amount of baggage, it was decided my luggage was the logical one to put the letters in. I found that a strange reward for having done something well; because I was good, I would be the one at risk. However, since none of our bags had been opened so far in the trip, I was not overly concerned.

Well, guess what? You guessed it. Only one suitcase was opened at the airport as we were leaving the country. Something on the x-ray flagged my suitcase, and the authorities grabbed it, asking me to step with them to a nearby table, where they ordered me to open it. I do not know what they were looking for, and could only watch as they rummaged through my things. In plain sight, visible for all to see, were about one hundred letters from people whose work would be in serious jeopardy if they were discovered. I watched the guards literally run their fingers through those letters, looking for something else. Not finding anything suspicious, they then told me to close my suitcase and proceed. I walked ahead with a deep sense of gratitude for God's providential care.

My transition from solely a local church growth focus to a world-wide kingdom growth outlook has been difficult for me, forcing me to leave my comfort zone often. Local church growth does not cause our doors to be pounded on in the midnight hour, nor does it cause our suitcases to be searched. Expanding our ministry vision comes at a cost. Few things of significance come easy, as progress almost always requires a willingness to run the risk of pain. When Jesus told us to take up our crosses, He meant it.

For my second trip, I had two advantages working for me. My wife and some church members would be with me. Also, Mary would be back in the country.

Our church graciously decided to pay for Ruth, my wife, to accompany me on my second trip. I personally needed Ruth to go with me for her to better understand this new love and commitment for missions that was pulsating through my system.

Ruth and I let it be known to our congregation we would be going to the foreign land, and this time we would visit our adopted unreached people group. We invited others to join us, but made no high pressure sales pitches. People should go overseas solely because God leads them to. Dangers and high costs should keep us from trying to force anyone to go. Some things are our responsibility, but others belong to God alone.

Five people, at great financial sacrifice to themselves, decided to join Ruth and me for the trip. We seven were met by our connection, Mary, in a coastal city. The eight of us then took off for the interior of the country. Our bus crossed two flooded bridges no bus driver in the United States would ever consider crossing. We had to climb by foot over a dangerous mudslide and find another bus on the other side to rent to finish our trip.

We stayed two nights in a government guest house, and were able to rent a Volkswagen mini-van to take us the last few miles of our trip. On a rainy day, we finally reached our destination, a village of our adopted unreached people group. It may sound corny, but is true nonetheless, I felt I had arrived home. I had carried these faceless, nameless people in my heart long enough for them to become mine—my daily prayer concerns, my responsibility.

We gave the children teddy bears we had brought from home. We bartered with women and children who surrounded us with wares to sell. The people ushered us to the heart of their village and presented a full tribal song and dance presentation.

Our adopted people group is one of the least evangelized groups of its size in the world. Of over three million people, only 10 are believers. People in other restricted areas usually have exchange students who come to the West and become believers. Our group, though, is totally isolated and insulated within the confines of their nation. They are a minority who receive little or no consideration from the people group which dominates their country. The gospel, for all intents and purposes, has never reached these people.

By God's grace, our church hopes to help change this sad fact. We are funding a translation of the *Jesus* film into their language, intend to pay for the translation of the New Testament into their language, and have a couple from our church living among them.

We already sense a moving of God among these dear people. Other countries and churches are sending help. Efforts are already afoot among at least six entities to place the gospel in these people's hands.

While in the village, I looked into one of their idol cages and prayed that someday these false gods would be replaced with a Bible paid for, as God enables, by our church. As we were leaving the village, our connection pointed to the only white building in sight, and said, "That's the wall I plan to show the *Jesus* film on someday." Again I thought, "by God's grace, paid for by our church."

The seven of us who made the trip have touched, seen, smelled, smiled at, bartered with, and walked among people who have never heard the name of Jesus. These people have never heard of New York City or Bethlehem. They know nothing of the United States or Israel, and worship evil spirits whom they dread.

We seven who stood among our people group will never be the same. Marilyn Murrow, an elementary school teacher, had felt a call to foreign missions as a teenager, but years and circumstances had made a response difficult. The renewed missions emphasis in our church and this trip overseas were "stirring the slumbering chords again." Old repressed memories were re-surfacing. She returned to our people group to teach English as a second language the next summer. She took along her daughter, a close friend, and church member, Elsie Boatright. Marilyn felt God calling her to full-time service among our adopted people group. She is currently serving on a long-term assignment.

Elsie Boatright is a senior citizen, a widow who once lived in Taiwan with her husband on a military detail. After he died, Elsie committed herself to traveling the world to do short-term volunteer missions projects. When her children expressed doubts and surprise at her resolve, she asked, "Did you think I would sit at home and quilt?" When they replied affirmatively, Elsie stood up, held out her hand, and said, "Well, shake hands with your new mom!" Elsie was our inspiration from the start of the trip. She returned with Marilyn in the summer to our people group.

Pam Patterson, an elementary school teacher, had never been outside the United States. We soon realized she was a natural with our people. They seemed drawn to her. She fared well on the trip, but did suffer a measure of culture shock. After the trip, she returned to our church choir, and in rehearsal one evening was singing along with a song which says, "I'll go, cross the rivers, cross the mountains, etc." She stopped in the middle of the song, and said to herself, "How often we don't have a clue as to what we are singing." Pam has already been involved in another mission trip from our church here in the United States, and she continues to participate in missions endeavors.

David Cavender, an engineer, handled all currency exchanges for us, provided much of the background information we needed for the trip, and lugged the video camera every mile of the trip. He is studying water projects, land use efforts, and construction needs as possible ways of helping to keep our foot in the door with our adopted people group. He has made a return trip and stays in constant touch with Mary regarding possible projects of this nature.

Bob Cirtin, an expert in detective work, is a college teacher who owns his own private investigating firm. His quick wit and seeming fearlessness in every given situation often proved a calming influence for our group. He developed a heart of compassion for Mary and has taken it upon himself to make sure we are doing all we can to meet her personal needs. For example, we paid for her to fly home to spend Christmas with her aged father, and for her to fly to be with us a few days to discuss strategy for our adopted people group.

Ruth returned from the trip with an overwhelming sense of blessing. "Why me to be born here," she asked, "and them to be born there?" One evening she said, "If I lived in a country where I suffered for my faith, I could only dream about a place of religious freedom. Imagine my horror if I learned such a country did exist, and that no one in that country had ever cared enough to try to come and tell me about a God who loved me enough to send His only Son to die for me."

The culminating event in the first two years of what we now call our missions revival was a world missions conference called Global Impact. This event was scheduled under the leadership of Global Focus. We brought to our church some 25 missionaries from every part of the world to meet with our people.

Global Impact was a totally new creation. It was not a world missions conference in the traditional sense. Missions conferences tend to be times when missionaries come to a church, share a few testimonies, and then head back to the field, with the church people responding by giving direct offerings of support to them or increasing giving to the denomination's missions cause.

In Global Impact, the missionaries are brought in to bond with small units in the church. Out of these small groups, which for us were Sunday school departments, partnerships are encouraged. A particular group becomes responsible for partnering with a given missionary. For instance, at our Global Impact, no missionary received an honorarium from our church at large. Instead, they received money and gifts from their partnering Sunday school classes. The guests stayed all night in people's homes, plus fellowshipped and prayed with class members. Already we have people designating gifts for the mission work of their particular missionary.

Out of some of these partnerships will grow church-wide efforts, maybe prayerwalking teams, construction workers, backyard Bible clubs, Vacation Bible Schools, revival teams, English teachers, etc. The possibilities seem almost endless.

On the first evening of Global Impact, we had a worship service in which every country represented by a missionary or visited by a group from our church in the last year was featured in a parade of flags. It was an emotional moment for "our seven" as we marched in under the flag of our adopted people group's country. Instead of being on the platform watching my people enter under the various flags, I was one of the people, coming in as one who had become involved in missions.

On the final night of Global Impact, 31 of our people surrendered to full-time ministry. Our people also pledged to give over twice as much to missions for the next year than they had ever given in any year before.

You may have noticed I have never referred in this story to the size of our church. This is intentional. Size does not matter. The Great Commission was given to every church, large and small. Not every church can do 10 or 20 mission projects a year. However, every church, without exception, can do a mission project every year in their Jerusalem, Judea, Samaria, and uttermost regions. In fact, every family and every individual can do this.

Christians want to obey their Master. They know they have a missions responsibility to the whole world, beginning next door. They simply need help. They need to catch a fresh new vision for the whole world, to see the possibilities laid out before us.

These are the most exciting days in the history of Christianity. More people are converting to our faith now than ever before. We have a duty to alert our people to what is happening and to provide resources for them to tap in to.

At our church, we like to use a visual image to portray what has happened among us. We tell our people we are setting the table for them. We are going to put on the tablecloth, prepare the silverware, put out the dishes, and even set the food before them. We are determined to take away from them every illegitimate excuse for not doing missions. If they don't participate, it is solely because they don't want to. We must make sure the responsibility for their inactivity is totally theirs.

After using this "setting the table" metaphor for months, we experienced an interesting climax to it. One of our speakers at Global Impact was Mike Stroope, a man who has trained hundreds of undercover workers. Unaware of the metaphor we had been using, Mike told the story of a time his daughter went forward in a public invitation. When Mike asked what she had done, the daughter said, "Dad, I'm putting my 'yes' on the table before God even asks."

CONSIDER THIS...

Should every church focus on at least one unreached people group? Why or why not?

Jesus said, "Go ye into all the world, and preach the gospel to every creature" (Mark 16:15). Should those who have never heard about salvation have priority over those who have often heard? Why or why not?

In the Great Commission, as given in Matthew 28:18-20, Jesus said we are to go because all power has been given to Him. Describe your prayers for the lost? Would you be willing to respond if God answered your prayers?

Paul said, "Pray without ceasing" (1 Thessalonians 5:17). How often do you pray for missions?

Write a prayer for undercover missionaries and for Christians who worship in secret due to fear of persecution.

What kind of sacrifice are you willing to make to go on mission trips?

Ruth asked, "Why me to be born here, and them to be born there?" How do you answer that question? Maybe God knew He would someday call you to go from here to there with His gospel?

CHAPTER 9

A CALL TO PRAYER

"HALLOWED BE THY NAME. THY KINGDOM COME.
THY WILL BE DONE IN EARTH, AS IT IS IN HEAVEN."

– Matthew 6:9d, 10

ANY EFFORT to fulfill the kingdom mission will utterly fail apart from prayer. Missions/evangelism is a pipe dream if not bathed in prayer. John Wesley well said, "God will do nothing but in answer to prayer."

My trips to see an unreached people group in a hostile Asian country shook something loose in me. Never have I felt such a burden, a burning desire, almost an obsession, to pray, to fall down in absolute submission before God. The Asia I saw looked utterly hopeless and helpless for ever receiving the kingdom of Christ.

After my two trips to Asia, a Scripture verse leaped from the pages of my Bible during my private time. Rarely has a passage hit me with such freshness. I trust it is a prediction of what will happen in the kingdom of God over the next several years as more and more Western believers increasingly focus their prayers on Asia.

Paul, after an experience in Asia similar to my own, wrote, "We do not want you to be unaware, brethren, of our affliction which came to us in Asia, that we were burdened excessively, beyond our strength, so that we despaired even of life" (2 Corinthians 1:8 NAS). I know what Paul was feeling. I, too, have been to Asia and sensed the despair.

Note Paul's response to his difficult Asian trip. "We had the sentence of death within ourselves in order that we should not trust in ourselves, but in God who raises the dead" (2 Corinthians 1:9 NAS). He felt so dead, so helpless, that he was absolutely compelled to turn from himself to God for strength. This has also been my response.

After his difficulty and being driven to prayer, Paul then made yet another response to Asia. "He will yet deliver us, you also joining in helping us through your prayers, that thanks may be given by many persons on our behalf for the favor bestowed upon us through the prayers of many" (2 Corinthians 1:10c, 11 NAS). Paul foresaw a day of victory in Asia.

Note the progression: After Asia, Paul was utterly forced to pray, but he believed his own prayers were not enough. He implored others to join him in prayer in order that God would receive widespread glory when their prayers were surely answered.

I pray we Christians in the West see here a foreshadowing of the next leg of our own collective spiritual pilgrimage. I, having gone to Asia, am being driven to prayer. Join me in concerted prayer for Asia, and as God pours upon us victory after victory, as He surely will, we shall collectively give Him all the honor and glory. Asia was for Paul and the church at Corinth a catalyst to pray. May it be the same for you, me, and the churches of our day.

As we turn our attention to the need for prayer, we focus on the Lord's Prayer. It is a wonderful prayer for kingdom advancement.

"HALLOWED BE THY NAME" (MATTHEW 6:9D)

"Hallowed" means set apart, reverenced. It is the opposite of profanity, dishonor, and disrespect. "Thy name" is a shorthand way of referring to all we know about God. He could have kept Himself hidden and secret, but in infinite condescension made Himself known. The fact He identified Himself to us at all is amazing. He let us know His "name," revealing Himself in ways discernible to us. "Hallowed be thy name" is a request for God to receive from mankind, the race to whom He graciously reveals Himself, all the profound reverence He deserves.

Many would probably admit they deem this the least meaningful phrase of the Lord's Prayer. We often glibly repeat the phrase without the slightest thought of its significance, but the fact that Jesus made it the first request in the Lord's Prayer speaks volumes about its importance. We need to ponder, why is this request first?

First, "Hallowed be thy name" takes priority due to the need for common courtesy. We need to begin prayer with our focus on

God, not on our selfish selves. Before we mention any concern about ourselves, let it be known our first concern is for Him.

As a young preacher I read Dale Carnegie's wonderful book, *How to Win Friends and Influence People.* It profoundly affected my ministry. One of the many courtesies it taught me is that being a good conversationalist requires talking about the other person. People love to talk about themselves. Thus, ask questions about their lives, talk about them. This simple act will cause us never to lack people who want to talk with us, for others will never consider us a bore or a bother.

This simple yet significant courtesy should be applied to God. Focus first on Him, not us. Applying this test to our prayers, we find we fail far too often. Remember, "prayer is not first of all a means by which we get something for ourselves; it is rather a method of helping God to get something for Himself" (G. Campbell Morgan). Our selfish praying often ties God's hands and thwarts His plans. When in prayer, ever be considering, what does God want?

Second, "Hallowed be thy name" takes priority because the evil it opposes is of epidemic proportions. The world at large does not reverence the true and living God. The vast majority do not believe in Him, and multitudes use the name of God and Jesus as oaths in anger or to accent a point. Even the church often stumbles at this point. A. W. Tozer said the greatest loss in the modern church was its loss of reverence for God. We sometimes use the Holy One as the punch-line of a joke, invoking God's name to provoke man's frivolity. This is not right.

Pray "hallowed be thy name, beginning in me." "Sanctify (same Greek root word as *hallowed)* the Lord God in your hearts" (1

Peter 3:15). I learned early on a good lesson about reverencing God. My mom, sister, brother, and I were one night watching on television a chorus line dancing to the song "When the Saints Go Marching In." Dad arrived home, saw what was on, immediately rushed to the TV, turned it off, and looking at us, said, "If I'd left that on one more minute, I'd be afraid God would strike our house with lightning," and then left the room. I do not recall hearing thunder that night, but I do remember learning something about the holiness of God. God is to be honored, hallowed, and reverenced within us all.

Third, "Hallowed be thy name" takes priority because the deepest need of humanity is a true knowledge of God. What one thinks of God affects everything else in a person's life.

A cruel god has cruel followers who tyrannize and terrorize others. They take hostages and bomb buildings, kill innocent children, and think they have done heaven a favor.

A god who demeans women and children will have devotees who do the same. Thus, often women are degraded and unwanted children are sent to orphanages as a convenient way to let them die and be dispensed with. In some countries women and children starve while cows deemed sacred walk the streets.

A licentious god has worshipers given to sexual squalor. A country whose gods are noted for sexual promiscuity has over two million male and female prostitutes, and one of earth's fastest growing AIDS rates.

An unknown god served in ignorance produces bewildered, frightened followers. In one country, when Christians began to succeed, witch doctors told the people they must cleanse the land of all that had been produced since the missionaries arrived. The people burned crops, and killed 400,000 head of cattle. As a result, 40,000 of their own people starved.

The best thing that could happen to this old, tired world would be for Jesus to become the one object of worship all the world over. Earth would be blessed if all its pagan deities fell into disrepute, and the One true God was exalted.

Multitudes have horrific, unworthy views of God. He deserves better; humanity needs better. We need a consuming passion for His reputation, a burning desire for the whole world to bow before God, for Him to be hallowed by every creature on earth.

People need to know the true God, the One full of love, holiness, and justice. Angels hallow God by saying "holy, holy, holy" in heaven. "Hallowed be thy name" is our request for the world to take up the chorus, for "holy, holy, holy" to fill the earth also.

"Hallowed be thy name" is the crying need of the world, and the needed cry of the church. Pray for this hallowing to begin in us, and then to spread from there. Not only must I hallow God, I must be an agent, an advocate, for others to do the same.

I find it significant that the Lord's Prayer's first request is a missionary request in the highest sense. The first order of business in any missionary enterprise is, "Hallowed be thy name." The modern missionary movement at times forgot this.

Some missionaries equated spreading the gospel with spreading Western culture. To become Christian, people were expected to change their dress, music, architecture, customs, and sometimes even their names.

Fortunately, today's missionaries are of a different bent. Pioneers plowed a different philosophy, one of accepting people as they are and of putting priority on hallowing God and not on becoming a Westerner.

The highest motive for missions must always be God's reputation. Ever seek for God's true self to be known. People need to see God as He is, for they can reverence Him, hallow His name, only if they know exactly what kind of God He is.

"Be still, and know that I am God: I will be exalted among the heathen, I will be exalted in the earth" (Psalm 46:10). "All nations whom thou hast made shall come and worship before thee, O Lord; and shall glorify thy name" (Psalm 86:9). When these verses were written, only one nation, Israel, had access to the living God. Now the gospel is indigenous to over ten thousand ethnolinguistic groups around the world. Having gone from one to ten thousand, Jesus' words, "Hallowed be thy name," still drive us forward to the 2,000 groups which remain unevangelized.

"THY" (MATTHEW 6:10A)

Do not overlook the significance of this second person possessive pronoun. We waste our time trying to promote God's kingdom if we are not first promoting the kingdom's God. Only if He is important to us will His kingdom be too. Until we are passionate for Him we will not be passionate for His work. In all we do, God must be first and foremost. He is everything.

We have long been told our motivation for missions/evangelism should be a burning, earnest compassion for the lost. People are going to hell, and we should care. This is certainly a legitimate and powerful motive for spreading the gospel, but the primary impetus for outreach must spring from a love for God.

Generating and sustaining a strong feeling of love for non-Christians is often difficult. "Love the lost" is a key phrase in our theological jargon, but in reality it is usually hard to feel deeply for a general population.

If we looked at a photograph of someone whom we had never met, we would find it hard to love that individual deeply. It is also hard to have and hold a deep abiding love for a nation, a people group, or a concept as nebulous as all non-Christians.

God can and does give us concern for unbelievers who are unknown to us, but the best way to foster evangelism and missions is to emphasize and improve our love for God, whom we do know firsthand. We should witness to neighbors primarily because Jesus died for them and He deserves the reward of His suffering. We should do missions around the world because God's precious Lamb shed His blood for all peoples and deserves to see benefits derived from His sacrifice.

The fountain of outreach must first spring from a heart in love with God. If we stumble over this word *thy*, the words "kingdom come" will impact us little.

"KINGDOM" (MATTHEW 6:10B)

God rules a moral and spiritual kingdom whose adherents give absolute allegiance solely to King Jesus. It is an inner kingdom, setting up its throne within the hearts of its citizens.

God's kingdom is not built on armies or earthly governments. It knows nothing of man-drawn boundaries, political entities, or time. All earthly kingdoms come and go, rise and fall, but God's kingdom ever abides. In every way, His kingdom is far greater than all the kingdoms of earth combined.

We should want God to rule over all hearts and minds, for this world's kingdoms leave us unfulfilled. In our world, woe and ruin abound. On every hand we see petty dictators, tyranny, and the strong crushing the weak. Women and children are dehumanized, and now Christians are the most persecuted group in the world.

This world-wide reign of pain and despair is not the kind of kingdom activity God ordains. Jesus wants all hurtful things removed. Look around at earth's anguish, and say, "This is not of God. An enemy has done this. Sin has invaded."

Each generation sees the problems of its day and, wanting something better, tries to lift the lot of humanity. Each generation offers its own new solution—communism, capitalism, social reform, education, science, civilization, politics, etc.

Each society thinks its new idea will be the one to save humanity; but as Alexander Maclaren once said, "Alas, alas! time after time the old experience is repeated, and the gratulations die down into gloomy silence." Hope persists, but disappointment repeats itself.

Never discourage people from dreaming of building a brighter future, but do encourage them to try what works. Man-made efforts help, but do not cure. This world's mind-set is always flawed. Only the kingdom of God can set things right.

Conditions can be bettered ultimately only by bettering individuals through giving them a new nature. The very nature of

God has to be implanted in them by a spiritual birth, as God's kingdom, this tired old world's best hope, expands on earth through the salvation of souls. Thus, pray for global evangelization, for people across the street and around the world. People need, more than all else, Jesus.

"COME" (MATTHEW 6:10C)

The fact we have to make the request proves the advance of God's kingdom is not automatic. There is opposition to overcome. Another spiritual kingdom is at work in this world. God's reign of penetrating light is resisted by Satan's reign of darkness.

God created this world to be His, but Satan seduced our race into a rebellion so successful that even the Bible calls him "the god of this world" (2 Corinthians 4:4). Satan sought to keep earth solely to himself, but God refused to abandon our race to the sinister foe. The whole drama of human history has been the epic struggle of God's progress in taking back this world.

God continues marching steadily forward, consistently reclaiming the peoples of earth for Himself. John saw in heaven "a great multitude, which no man could number, of all nations, and kindreds, and people, and tongues" (Revelation 7:9). This foreshadowed God's inevitable victory in His irresistible movement to be known in every corner of Satan's usurped territory.

Be assured Satan resists the advance of God's kingdom at every hand. The battle is engaged. We will never understand prayer until we are mindful of the fact that this cosmic war ceaselessly rages in microcosm in each and every one of our hearts.

Paul understood this reality. He grasped the dynamic at work. He "fought a good fight" (2 Timothy 4:7), and commanded us to "fight the good fight of faith" (1 Timothy 6:12). He told us to wear "armor" (Ephesians 6:11), not pajamas or formal evening wear.

Life is war. "Our weakness in prayer is owing largely to our neglect of this truth. Prayer is primarily a wartime walkie-talkie for the mission of the church as it advances against the powers of darkness and unbelief. It is not surprising that prayer malfunctions when we try to make it a domestic intercom to call upstairs for more comforts in the den" (John Piper, *Let the Nations Be Glad,* Grand Rapids: Baker, 2003, 41. Used by permission.).

Pray for victory in this ultimate war. Look at our lost neighbors and silently pray, "Thy kingdom come." Weep over lost kin and plead, "Thy kingdom come." Think of the world's unreached peoples and beg, "Thy kingdom come." In every situation where we confront the kingdom of lostness, pray, "Thy kingdom come." Herein we find victory. Someone once said prayer is striking the winning blow, service is gathering up the results. Let us pray, flooding heaven with our wartime walkie-talkie, and then go forth in missions/evangelism to harvest the results.

"THY WILL BE DONE" (MATTHEW 6:10D)

Only four words, yet this small treasure chest holds at least two precious diamonds of truth. First, "Thy will be done" reminds us God's will can be known. It would be a mockery of humanity if God told us to do His will, but never told us what His will is. God's will, His desires, plans, and purposes for us, can be known.

In the Bible, He articulates His will in words easily understood—very clear and very straightforward.

From the beginning, God has ruled His people by revealing and preserving His will on the printed page. When God first brought Israel out of Egypt, He led them by Moses, who took pen in hand to write the first five books of the Bible.

Joshua wrote God's will, as did Samuel, David, Solomon, and the prophets. Jesus in His own life on earth flawlessly fleshed out the will of God. Of this perfect expression of God's will, Matthew wrote, Mark wrote, Luke wrote, John wrote, Paul wrote. The Son inerrantly embodied the Father's will; the Holy Spirit inerrantly wrote the Father's will. We possess written in print the Father's intentions for us.

God's will can be known, and we begin to learn it by knowing God's Book, the Bible. Daily read in it; learn it; memorize it; meditate on it; cherish it.

Second, "Thy will be done" teaches us God's will must be obeyed. It is not enough to know it, we must also do it. God's will must become the standard for human actions, beginning in us. Pray, "Thy will be done, and be done first in me."

Doing God's will is the most important activity in the world. We usually speak of Jesus' life in terms of what He came to do for us, but Jesus often said He came to do His Father's will. He was obsessed first of all with pleasing His Father.

The will of the Father is what matters most. We must know it and do it, and then give ourselves to helping others know it and do it. To pray "Thy will be done" is to pray for a yielded spirit in ourselves and others. This is thus another prayer for gospel success, for conversion of non-Christians, for the missions/evangelism enterprise.

"Thy will be done" brings us to the nitty gritty work of the outreach task of the church. Prayer is indispensable and its importance to our expansion efforts cannot be overemphasized. Yes, prayer is the power source, but not the task. Prayer is the wind in our sails, but not the ship. The actual spreading of God's will requires that the object of our prayers be definite strategies, not nebulous wishes or vague conceptions.

To illustrate, I again use the "life is war" motif. A cardinal rule of warfare is, "To win a war, one has to occupy." In other words, a nation can be truly subdued only if ground troops are sent in to occupy it after the battles end. "To win a war, one has to occupy" is also a spiritual truism. God's will can be done long-term only in a person or region that has been occupied. This simply means the Bible, the ultimate expression of God's will, must become integral to a person or indigenous to a place. Without the Bible, new converts shrivel. Without the Bible, churches fade into oblivion, as in liberal protestantism.

Without the Bible, the Arab world was snatched from Christianity by Islam. In that era, people had Scripture in Latin, but it had not been translated into languages of the Middle East and North Africa. Thus, when false doctrine came, people had no concrete truths to hold on to. The land had not been occupied and our loss was grievous.

We need to pray specifically for the Bible to be translated and distributed in all the earth. "Thy will be done" totally depends on the Word of God becoming an integral part of a person or region's life. Otherwise, our missions/evangelism prayers are vain, and the kingdom advance is aborted before it takes root.

The Word is what matters. Acts equates the success of church growth with the success of the Word. "The word of God increased and the number of disciples multiplied greatly" (6:7). "The word of God grew and multiplied" (12:24). "The word of the Lord spread through all that region" (13:49). "The word of the Lord grew and prevailed mightily" (19:20).

The church has finally caught on. The Bible, available in Jesus' day in only two languages, Hebrew and Greek, is now the world's most translated book, available in whole or in part in over 1,500 languages. We learned that to win we must occupy.

A second cardinal rule of warfare is that to occupy, one must penetrate. Someone has to break through enemy lines, and open up the way. For non-Christians to be "occupied" by the will of God, Christians have to make it happen. A believer must take the Word to unbelievers next door. A missionary or a mission team must take the Word overseas. Someone has to do the work of penetrating, of going in with the Word, which has the power to "occupy," to make the results last.

When praying for God's will to be done, pray specifically for the Word to occupy and for messengers to penetrate. Paul, the greatest extender of our faith ever, realized both were essential, and combined them in his prayer requests. He pleaded, "Pray for us, that the word of the Lord may spread rapidly" (2 Thessalonians 3:1 NAS). He asked prayer for God to "open up to us a door for the word" (Colossians 4:3 NAS).

China and the United States, the two countries with the most evangelical Christians, illustrate the importance of occupation and penetration. Christianity entered China in the Middle Ages, but soon totally disappeared. Missionaries did not stay long, and the Bible was not translated into Chinese. No occupation and no penetration led to failure.

In the 1800s missionaries returned to China to stay a century, and the Bible was translated into Chinese. In 1949 the communists expelled missionaries and tried to eradicate Bibles, but it was too late, their country had been occupied and penetrated, resulting in over one million conversions a year for the next 55 years.

In the mid-1600s, the Puritan pastor John Trapp challenged his congregation, "Let us also pity and pray for such poor souls in Asia and America as worship the devil." Fortunately the Puritans did more than solely pray. Between 1627 and 1640, 15,000 of them emigrated from England to America to bring the will of God to our shores. The seal of the Massachusetts Bay colonists had on it a Native American, saying, "Come over into Macedonia and help us" (Acts 16:9). They penetrated; they brought the Word to occupy, and their legacy has lasted.

As we pray "Thy will be done," be not content with only general terms such as "Lord, save my neighbors and folks overseas." Pray instead for a specific strategy, "Lord, Thy will be done next door and around the world. Make Your will known to them by raising up emissaries, beginning with me." "Thy will be done" will remain a powerless request until we ourselves are willing to take the Bible message and put it in people's hands so they can know and do the Father's will.

"IN EARTH" (MATTHEW 6:10E)

Life is war. God expects us to penetrate the kingdom of darkness, taking in His Word that it may occupy a land. The Spirit pierces hearts and brings conviction, using as His sword the Bible, which then remains as the rule and law of life.

God wants to govern the whole earth by His Word. He has a specific will He desires to see fulfilled by every human being. The Lord is serious about what happens on earth. He is earnest about His revealed will being the paramount determiner of human conduct.

This surprises many. Throngs in our culture bow at the altar of moral relativism, worshiping the idea people are free to decide for themselves what is right and wrong. We live in a society which increasingly rejects the fact of moral absolutes. All things are deemed relative, as if to say: IF there is a God, He does not have any absolute moral standards; He is quite laid back about human behavior, and people are on their own to choose how they will act.

Wrong! Our text goes against this deviant grain of our culture. God is not lackadaisical. He has specific desires He wants enacted. He has plans and purposes He wants fulfilled. In other words, God takes His Godness very seriously. Since this is true, since it is a fact God is very serious about being God, then nothing else in the world is as important as knowing and doing what He wills. God wants to rule all the earth, and every human being in it, by His Word. Be wise. Obey Him.

"AS IT IS IN HEAVEN" (MATTHEW 6:10F)

Prayer should begin with seeking what God wants, and a main emphasis in prayer should be to plead for earth to become a world in which God can feel at home. We have a prototype to shape our prayers. We should pray for earth to become like heaven, a place where God, feeling at home, rules without opposition.

In heaven, God's will is done fully. There are no pockets of resistance. No closet or corner hides defiance. The Father's will is done in every nook and cranny of heaven. Sadly, we cannot say the same of earth. This is why David Bryant is right in saying every believer should be a "world Christian." Not every Christian is called to be a home or foreign missionary, but every believer is expected to be a world Christian, one who prays and labors for God's name to be hallowed in every corner of the globe, for God's kingdom to come from pole to pole and sea to sea, for God's will to be done in every continent, country, county, city, and citizen of earth.

A limited perspective by Christians is a major hindrance to the spread of Christianity. Refuse to relinquish any square inch of territory to the devil. God deserves to rule everyone everywhere on earth. He has all of heaven; let's not rest until He also has all of earth. Not all will be saved, but prayer and painstaking effort will win many.

In heaven, God's will is done quickly. There is no reluctance, never a moment's hesitation. Angels are characterized by entire submission of their will to God. They are thus constantly ready to do His bidding. Jesus portrayed them as ever looking at the Father's face (Matthew 18:10), the picture being one of readiness to fulfill God's commands. They are anxious to know in order to go. They remain ever on the wing, as it were, angels of light ready to respond at the speed of light.

Unfortunately, on earth there are contrary wills which seek to impede God's will. Satan's will resists God's, as often do our own will and the will of family and friends. Learn to obey God quickly.

Hasten to do His will. Give it priority over all other wills combined. Do not hesitate. We should be in the habit of freely and quickly bending our wills in whatever direction He chooses.

In heaven, God's will is done gladly. There is no regret, no remorse. Everyone not only does the will of God; they actually enjoy doing it. There is on earth no height of holiness higher than fully and quickly doing God's will. When we also gladly do His will, we are elevated to walking in the suburbs of heaven itself.

I fear we often are not as vigilant as we should be about this aspect of the Christian life. We sometimes sing as if we are sick, pray as if anemic, and preach or listen to sermons as if bored. Such dreary routine mocks real obedience.

The greatest saints have always been those who revel in doing God's will, who intensely enjoy it. They deem it a delight, not a drudgery or burden. David said, "I delight to do thy will, O my God" (Psalm 40:8). Jesus confessed, "My food is to do the will of Him who sent Me" (John 4:34 NAS). A pioneer missionary once said, "There is no greater joy than saving souls." And others lived extraordinarily arduous, sacrificial lives, yet two wrote, "I never made a sacrifice."

God's light shines brightest through us when our duty becomes our delight. "God is most glorified in us when we are most satisfied in Him" (John Piper, *Let the Nations Be Glad,* Grand Rapids: Baker, 2003, 42. Used by permission.).

In heaven, God's will is done fully, quickly, and gladly. Pray for the same to be done here on earth. We are not to wait until we get to heaven to do God's will. We have tasks to accomplish here that angels themselves are unable to do. We will in heaven have work to do and service to perform, but only on earth can we win non-Christians, help the poor, lift up the fallen, and relieve the downtrodden.

Heaven has no slums, no homeless people, no families living on a garbage dump, no single moms struggling to survive. There are ministries to fulfill here on earth which are so wonderful that an argument could almost be made for their being nearly as worthwhile as the works done in heaven itself. We can accomplish things angels can only dream of, and the saints in heaven can only reminisce about. Charles Spurgeon once said, "If we did but live as we should live, we might make Gabriel stoop from his throne and cry, 'I wish I were a man!'" We on earth are in the arena. Let us rise to do God's will, to tackle those missions we can fulfill only while on earth.

CONSIDER THIS...

Are your prayers for missions done solely out of a sense of duty? Explain your motivations.

In your opinion, why is the phrase "Hallowed be thy name" usually underestimated?

Do you believe Jesus is the best hope for this world? If so, what are you doing to help make it happen?

What evidence of resistance to kingdom advance do you regularly see?

Is your church involved in Bible translation work? Should it be?

What do you need to do on earth that you will not be able to do in heaven?

Read Matthew 6:9. Did Jesus intend the Lord's Prayer to be a missions prayer? Explain.

Read Matthew 6:10. Is it okay to pray this prayer without seeking to be part of our own answer to it? When asking for God's kingdom to come, should we be seeking to extend it ourselves?

CHAPTER 10

YES, LORD

"SEEK YE FIRST THE KINGDOM OF GOD."

– Matthew 6:33a

LIFE'S MAIN BUSINESS is God's business, the enterprise of extending His kingdom. Life's ultimate urgency and highest priority is to spread the rule of God into the hearts of as many people as possible. Our primary desire should be for God to win over evil in us, in our neighbors, our state, our country, and our world whatever the personal cost.

This driving force within is essential to our success because reaching others always costs. For Christ, a world view meant wounds, blood, mocking, nakedness, rejection. For us it will mean heartache, time, agonizing prayer, money. This is no small commitment, but when we become burdened for the world we will be more like Jesus on the cross than we will ever be otherwise. If we truly love Him, we will want to be like Him. This is what enabled the disciples to do what they did. They loved Jesus more than anything else in the whole world. They were sold out to Him. He was the obsession of their lives. Nothing was as important as pleasing and imitating Him.

The obsession needed for God's kingdom was shown in Paul's determination to run the risk of preaching in Jerusalem, a city where many wanted him dead. Paul's friends, knowing his life would be in peril, begged him not to go, but he was determined, "None of these things move me, neither count I my life dear unto myself" (Acts 20:24). Food, clothing, and life meant little. Later his friends again tried to convince him, but Paul replied, "What are you doing, weeping and breaking my heart? For I am ready not only to be bound, but even to die at Jerusalem for the name of the Lord Jesus." Paul was adamant, and Luke wrote, "Since he would not be persuaded, we fell silent, remarking, 'The will of the Lord be done!'" (Acts 21:13,14 NAS). What mattered most to Paul was extending God's kingdom, whatever the personal cost.

The time is right for local churches to accelerate their efforts to seek first the kingdom of God. This is our moment. When Queen Esther wavered due to fear for her life, hesitating to confront the king on behalf of her people, Mordecai tried to embolden her by encouraging her to grasp her God-given moment of destiny, "Who knoweth whether thou art come to the kingdom for such a time as this?" (Esther 4:14). She responded to this challenge courageously, sending word to Mordecai, "So will I go in unto the king, which is not according to the law: and if I perish, I perish" (Esther 4:16).

Who knows? Maybe the churches in America have come to the kingdom for such a time as this. Who knows? Maybe some among us are being called to perish for the cause. We have to leave to God the determining of consequences. Our duty is to commit ourselves to the kingdom of God first, to answer His call with reckless abandon.

At this point you have every right to ask, "John, be specific; exactly what do you think is expected of us?" Rather than garble my answer with generalities, I will seek to be clear and precise. Let us give ourselves no rest until we each find our four niches in God's kingdom. We each have a niche in our hearts where we commune with the King; use it daily. We each have a niche in our own local church, inside the barracks; find where we are to use our spiritual gifts within the local church to help our fellow believers. We each have a niche in our home town; we are to be evangelizing, witnessing locally. We each have a niche in our Judea (our state) and our Samaria (our country) and our uttermost part of the earth; we should all be involved somehow somewhere in missions.

I pray we each would find our four niches in the kingdom of God's invasion of the kingdom of darkness. Before D-Day, Allied troops amassed in Britain. Hitler later said America and Britain were the only two countries in history who could have trusted each other enough to accomplish such an invasion. The British risked everything, trusting we would not leave our troops as an occupying force on their soil. As the troops gathered, they individually had no idea where they would be sent in the attack, to Omaha Beach,

Utah Beach, or some other point of invasion. Their task was merely to report for duty and await directions. Sounds like Christians of our day. Report for duty and await directions.

Are we willing to risk listening to God or are we afraid of what we might hear? Can we say, "To help God's kingdom invade the darkness, I am willing to prayerwalk my block and test the waters to see if God might open a door for me to win my neighbors. I am willing to learn about my state, my country, the world."

At the core of our being there has to be a huge "yes" to whatever God may say. This can happen only if our desire is to seek the kingdom of God first.

Kingdom success is found in yielding to God's service everything, every ounce of our being, every person we know, every possession we own. My boyhood idol was Mickey Mantle. His teammate Bobby Richardson, a devoted Christian, often tried to win Mickey to faith. Fortunately, not long before Mickey died, Bobby's efforts succeeded. At a Fellowship of Christian Athletes' meeting, Bobby once prayed a classic prayer: "Dear God, Your will—nothing more, nothing less, nothing else, Amen." Pray often, "Lord, all I am, all I have, it's yours. What do You want me to do with it?"

The Moravian Brethren's missionary emblem shows an ox standing between a plow and an altar. Under the picture are the words "Ready for either!" Here is the true spirit of Christ: ready to live or die; ready to serve or sacrifice—whatever God requires.

Having heard Dad speak often of being a mule-farmer, I have developed a mental picture of myself as being not a thoroughbred, but a plow-horse. I envision an old, faithful horse who knows his master's voice and touch. Every day, before plowing, the work horse stands under a shade tree by the field to be plowed and listens to his master's will. The horse, hitched to the plow, drags it faithfully down a row, looking neither right nor left, making a perfect, straight furrow. This pictures service, but some days the call is to sacrifice on the altar something we own or someone we know. The call may someday be for our lives. We must yield to this duty as willingly as we have to taking the plow every day.

Total surrender of our all to God must be our first priority in every endeavor. Seek God's kingdom first, holding nothing back. We must be willing to pour out our lives in service for God's kingdom. Elisha Hoffman's old hymn ("Is Your All on the Altar," 1900) still needs to be sung.

> Is your all on the altar of sacrifice laid?
> Your heart, does the Spirit control?
> You can only be blest and have peace and sweet rest,
> As you yield Him your body and soul.

We have to ask ourselves repeatedly, are we merely playing games, or is God's kingdom truly the most important enterprise in the cosmos? His cause cries out for citizens who are earnest about it.

Nearing death, George Whitefield could think of only one thing, the cause. He prayed, "Lord Jesus, I am weary in Thy work, but not of it. If I have not yet finished my course, let me go and speak for Thee once more in the fields, seal Thy truth, and come home to die!" That night, in his last sermon, he preached, "How willingly would I live forever to preach Christ. But I die to be with Him." Within hours he was in heaven.

As a young man, John Wesley began spending two hours a day in private devotions. He wrote his mother, "Leisure and I have parted company." A biographer later added, "And they never met again." At 87 he wrote, "I am now an old man. My eyes are dim. My right hand shakes very much. But blessed be God, I do not slack my labor. I can still preach and write."

I urge us to spare no pain in seeking God's kingdom first, for anything less than absolute diligence will end in futility and defeat. Our only hope at success in the kingdom enterprise is to pursue it above all else.

Obstacles await us. We live in enemy territory and carry a traitor in our own breast. Laggardly slackness will not avail. If we are not seeking God first, I fear we are for all practical intents not seeking Him at all. What one seeks first reveals one's essential character. Jesus is either Lord of all or not Lord at all.

Except for William Carey, perhaps no person has had a wider impact on the modern mission movement than James Hudson Taylor. He began the "interior" movement, the drive to take the gospel inland, away from the coasts where Christian influences were already felt. In some ways he is the grandfather of our modern unreached peoples movement.

Before Taylor was born, his parents knelt to dedicate their first child to God. At age 17, James Hudson became a Christian. "Well do I remember," he wrote later, "as in unreserved consecration I put myself, my life, my friends, my all upon the altar. . . . A deep consciousness that I was not my own took possession of me . . . I felt I was in the presence of God." A voice spoke to his heart, "Go for Me to China!" His commitment to China never wavered from that moment. He began teaching himself to read Chinese characters, and gave himself to winning others to Christ, believing he had to be a soulwinner at home before he could be one abroad.

To prepare for the rigors of missionary life, Taylor gave up as many creature comforts as possible. He disposed of his feather-bed and began sleeping on the floor every night. He moved out of his comfortable home into an apartment measuring less than 12 feet square. He ate oatmeal, rice, and brown bread; paid his small rent, and gave the rest of his income to God's work.

When the beautiful music teacher he loved would not consent to go to China with him, it was a perilous moment. He gave her up, but his grief was almost unbearable. His faith in God was severely tested. He could not understand why. The devil for days tempted him to give up his ministry and return to the lady, but at last, the Great Physician began to heal his broken heart. "God does not deprive me of feeling in my trial," James wrote his sister, "yet He enables me to sing."

Then came the parting from his mother. On the boat the two of them and two friends read a psalm, sang a song, and prayed a prayer. "While we waved our handkerchiefs," his mother later wrote friends, "he took his stand at the head, afterwards climbed into the rigging, waving his hat, looking more like a victorious hero, than a stripling just entering the battlefield. Then his figure became less and less distinct, and in a few moments passenger and ship were lost to sight."

"Victorious hero" indeed, off to live a life which altered the course of Christian history, an answer to his prayer for "widespread usefulness." His daughter died, son died, wife died, second wife died, but the call to China never wavered. Extending the kingdom took priority in his life.

Seek God's kingdom first. Horatio Spafford (1876) wrote my favorite song, "It Is Well With My Soul," after his daughters were drowned at sea. His wife survived that disaster and wired her husband, "Saved alone." The first word was pleasant; the second word dreadful. As God strengthens us, I pray when we someday stand before the King and answer for how we helped spread the kingdom, may none of us have to say, "Saved alone."

OUR STORY

A few years ago I felt I was in the bleachers, far away from the action down on the field. The commissioning voice of Jesus was but a faint echo. Today, though, I feel I am standing on home plate. I easily pretend Jesus is again giving the Great Commission. I hear Him say, "Peter, you need to go to the Jews. You'll do your best work there." Jesus then turns to me and says, "John, do you have some people in your church who will link arms with several agencies and other churches in your city to help with My work there?"

"Yes, Lord, I think I can find some members to help in our Jerusalem." As I begin to leave, I hear Jesus say, "Andrew, you've always been bringing people to me. Carry on."

After getting people started on "Jerusalem" assignments, I return to the batter's box and hear Jesus say, "John, could you enlist some folks to help with the Forest Avenue Homeless Shelter in Kansas City; and how about the Winnebago Reservation and Schuyler Hispanic Church in Nebraska?"

"Yes, Lord, I believe we can find people interested in that." As I trot off to the dugout to enlist the workers, I hear Jesus say, "James, I'll need you in Jerusalem. Time may be short. Stay faithful. Work hard while there's time."

Returning to home plate, I hear Jesus say, "John, good to see you again. Do you have some tenderhearted saints who would go to Montana for me; and how about Chicago?"

"Yes, Lord, I never would have thought of that on my own, but now that You mention it, yes, I do think we have folks willing to do that." As I run off to muster the troops, I hear Jesus saying, "John, my beloved, you'll have to go to Patmos. I'll give you more instructions there."

As I return to the batter's box, I hear Jesus call, "John." What an honor to know He is talking to me. "Yes, Lord." "John, how about Mexico, Spain, Nepal? . . ." I feel my mind drifting, wondering how in the world we can do this. Jesus, not seeming to notice my reticence, continues, "Oh, yes, I'll need a few folks in Belarus and Asia. By the way, John, you have enough doctors and nurses in your church to start a hospital. Do you think a few of them would be willing to go to Tanzania for Me? Would you talk to them about it?"

"Yes, Lord, I think I can do that." As I run to my teammates, I hear Jesus telling Thomas, "I'll need you to go to India for me." Thomas didn't know for sure where India was, but was willing to go anyway.

Back at home plate, I felt Jesus put His arm around my shoulder. The soft tone in His voice alerted me to the fact His next commission would be special. As we walked a few steps together, He quietly spoke, "John, I have a people group in a hostile country that needs to hear the gospel. They've never heard My name. Would you go to them for Me?"

"Sure, Lord, I have people willing to go."

"No, John, I need you yourself to go." I feel His arm tightening around my shoulder.

"But, Lord, others can do better than I can. I don't travel well. I don't want to be away from Ruth. I . . ."

"Son," Jesus interrupts as we walk, "You have more Christians present at your family reunions than I have followers in this people group. John, will you go?"

There's really no choice to make. To be in the game, you have to be willing to play.

"John, will you take the gospel where it has never been taken before?"

With reluctance now gone, assent swells forth, "Yes. Yes! YES!"

Right when I should be experiencing a mid-life crisis, God has placed a surge of enthusiasm in my life. Ruth and I are not slowing down, we are putting our feet on the accelerator and pushing harder and with more excitement than ever before. Ruth, our church, and I are no longer on the sidelines. We're now in the middle of the action, on the cutting edge of the Great Commission.

CONSIDER THIS...

What would it cost you to become sold-out for missions?

Are you more concerned about doing your duty or about possible consequences it might cause?

At the core of your being, is there a huge "yes!" to whatever God may say? Explain.

Are you in danger of having to enter heaven with "saved alone" as your testimony? If so, what changes can you make?

Read Matthew 6:33. How can we know for sure we are seeking God's kingdom first? How would we know if it isn't first in our lives?

Read Acts 21:13, 14. Why would God ever expect any of us to pay the ultimate cost, to give up life itself, in order for lost people to hear the gospel?

THE WORLD VIEW DOCUMENT
FULFILLING THE DREAM, ONE STEP AT A TIME

IN EARLY 1997, Second Baptist Church (Springfield, Missouri) was entering its third consecutive year of remarkable growth. As pastor, I was pleased but also concerned that we weren't doing as well in global outreach as we were locally. Missions did not seem as important to us as church growth.

I began sharing my concern with our staff. They decided we should convene a group of church leaders to meet once a week for several weeks to discuss how the implications and examples found in Acts 1–13 should be affecting a local church today. We chose this passage because its stories and lessons covered the gamet of a church's outreach responsibilities locally and globally.

Our staff compiled a list of 100 key leaders for this missions discussion group. We called them the World Viewers. I met with them on Wednesday night for several weeks. The result of these deliberations was a set of concrete, measurable missions goals we compiled into a report called the World View Document.

After much discussion and input, our church as a whole voted unanimously to adopt and implement the World View Document. It became the blueprint, guiding what we would later call "The Missions Revival at Second."

This approach to developing a church's mission strategy could be very effective in any church. The process begins with pastor and staff convening a missions discussion group. This allows church leaders to lead, to make a statement on the importance of missions, and to set the example for others to follow.

A discussion group allows laypeople to have huge input in the plan. If missions is going to have a top priority in our churches, lay people will be required to carry the bulk of the load. Therefore, it is only fair and appropriate for them to provide input from the beginning.

A church vote brings focus for the church, and places authority on the plan. Every church member is privy to all details of the plan, and knows this plan is the church's guiding blueprint for missions because it has been adopted in an official business session.

Below is a copy of our World View Document. Use it as an example and template for your ministry. If your church does not participate, set your own personal goals in obedience to the Great Commission. Be an encouragement and an example.

THE WORLD VIEW DOCUMENT

Our Master's mandate is clear, "But ye shall receive power, after that the Holy Ghost is come upon you: and ye shall be witnesses unto me both in Jerusalem, and in all Judea, and in Samaria, and unto the uttermost part of the earth" (Acts 1:8).

UTTERMOST

Our vision for the uttermost parts of the earth is to seek to fulfill our Master's command by being His witnesses to every continent on earth.

USA

Under the leadership of the Holy Spirit our vision is to faithfully and systematically involve every member of our church in furthering the cause of Christ in the four geographic areas of the United States of America, our Samaria, in mission activity through prayer, finances, and personal involvement.

STATE

Our vision for our state, our Judea, is to initiate, facilitate, and/or nurture works in every part of our state which help meet the spiritual, physical, emotional, financial, and social needs of people.

CITY

Our vision for our city, our Jerusalem, is to initiate, facilitate, and/or nurture works for people of all ages, backgrounds, and needs in every part of the city, by providing help spiritually, physically, emotionally, financially, and socially.

TO ACCOMPLISH THIS VISION, IN 20 YEARS WE SHALL:

UTTERMOST

- Sponsor at least one mission church on every continent on earth.

USA

- Sub-groups from our sub-groups to send out people to do mission projects.
- Have a minimum of eight mission points in the four geographic areas.

STATE

- Trust the works we have helped will be helping other works.

CITY

- Have established a cooperative key church partnership with six churches. The key church strategy is a process through which associations, state conventions, and the North American Mission Board establish cooperative relationships with churches to facilitate evangelism, ministry, and church planting as top priorities.
- Have Bible studies, child care, and worship services within 20 apartment complexes with 20 missionaries. This ministry is designed to plant Bible studies, child care, and worship services within several apartment communities in the city.

BY 15 YEARS WE SHALL:

UTTERMOST

- Sponsor at least one church on each of four continents.

USA

- Have a minimum of six mission points in the four geographic areas.
- Have a financial goal of $500,000 for mission work in the United States in addition to the mission offering.
- Involve at least 10 other churches in mission activity training.

STATE

- We shall have helped a work in each of the congressional districts in our state.

CITY

- Have established a cooperative key church partnership with four churches.
- Have personally contacted 100 percent of teachers and administrators in public schools indicating our prayer support for them. "Adopt a School" is a prayer support ministry designed to encourage and support faculty in all public schools.
- Have established Bible studies, child care, and worship services within 10 apartments with 10 missionaries.

BY 10 YEARS WE SHALL:

UTTERMOST

- Sponsor at least one church on each of three continents.

USA

- Get adult/college/youth Sunday school departments individually involved in sending out/sponsoring mission projects.
- Involve at least five other churches in mission activity training.
- Set a goal of $30,000 for Easter offering for North American missions.
- Establish the fourth mission point in fourth geographic area.

STATE

- We shall have helped a work in each of the geographic districts in our state.

CITY

- Have established a cooperative key church partnership with three churches.
- Have personally contacted 75 percent of teachers and administrators in our city's public schools indicating our prayer support for them.
- Have established Bible studies, child care, and worship services within five apartments with five missionaries.

BY 5 YEARS WE SHALL:

UTTERMOST

- Sponsor at least one church on each of two continents.

USA

- Send 200 people on mission projects within the United States.
- Send and fully fund five student summer missionaries from our church.
- Develop an emergency disaster team.
- Develop a church construction team.
- Establish a third mission point in a third geographic area.
- Send out our first career home missionary.
- Set a goal of $25,000 for the Easter offering for North American missions.
- Develop first mission church.
- Involve one other church in mission activity training.
- Establish training teams to send to mission points.

STATE

- We shall have helped a work in the state's capital city.

CITY

- Have established a cooperative key church partnership with two churches.
- Have personally contacted 40 percent of teachers and administrators in our city's public schools indicating our prayer support for them.
- Have established Bible studies, child care, and worship services within two apartments with two missionaries.

ON DECEMBER 31, 3 YEARS, WE SHALL:

UTTERMOST
- Present to the church a detailed strategy, targeting specific assignments for subcongregations.

USA
- Report to the church, reassessing what we have done.

STATE
- Report to the church, reassessing what we have done.

CITY
- Report to the church, reassessing what we have done.

BY 4 YEARS WE SHALL:

UTTERMOST
- Have a world Missions Conference, hosting several foreign missionaries.

USA
- Develop an ongoing revival team (preacher, music leader, music ensemble).
- Have 150 persons involved in mission projects.
- Set a goal of $20,000 for the Easter offering for North American missions.

- Sponsor and fully fund four college student summer missionaries.
- Have one short-term missionary.

STATE
- Help at least one work in a specified area of our state, and one church in another area of the state.

CITY
- Have entered negotiations with one church in our city to establish a cooperative key church partnership.
- Have personally contacted 20 percent of teachers and administrators in our city's public schools indicating our prayer support for them.
- Have entered into negotiations with a large apartment complex in the city and laid the ground work to rent and place one missionary in that apartment by the end of _____.

IN 3 YEARS WE SHALL:

UTTERMOST
- Increase giving by one percent.

USA
- Continue the youth ministry mission point currently established.
- Establish a second mission point in a separate geographic area.
- Implement mission projects at mission points, including the second point established.

- Have 100 persons involved in mission projects.
- Sponsor and fully fund two college student summer missionaries.
- Set a goal of $15,000 for the Easter offering for North American missions.

STATE

- Help a work in our city.

IN 2 YEARS WE SHALL:

UTTERMOST

- Seek to give the largest Christmas offering for World Missions in our church's history. We will henceforth endeavor to give each year more than the year before.
- On October _____, we will host a Global Focus seminar.
- On May _____, we will open negotiations with our International Mission Board about an unreached people group.
- On November _____, we will evaluate progress. World Viewers will be responsible for evaluation.

USA

- Seek to enlist a Minister of USA Missions to serve on our church staff.
- Establish a USA Missions Task Force to work with Minister of USA Missions.
- Sponsor and fully fund one college student summer missionary.

STATE

- Help a church near ours.
- Evaluate progress in November _____. World Viewers will be responsible for evaluation.

CITY

- Have enlarged the scope of "Least of These" ministries by providing spiritual, financial, material, personnel, human resource, and awareness support to this ministry. "Least of These" is a church ministry designed to make aware, support, and promote our city's numerous crisis and need-related service organizations.
- Be the primary sponsor of a city-wide college ministry focusing on Bible study, praise, and worship. This weekly gathering is designed to meet the needs of the nearly 30,000 college students in our city's area.
- Have conducted Backyard Bible Clubs in 25 different locations across the area. Our goal is to support these Bible Clubs for future growth and expansion throughout the next 23 years. This "Love-Link" ministry will focus on child evangelism.
- Begin a mall ministry, having entered negotiations with mall officials to determine possible outreach ministry opportunities (for example, music groups playing and singing during seasonal activities, free gift wrapping, child care, car window washing, etc.).
- Have laid the ground work for a School of Fine Arts and outreach programs such as a concert artist series and a lecture series. This ministry is designed to reach people of every age and cultural background through the fine arts.

THROUGH THE EYES OF **GOD**

NOTE TO LEADERS

AS A LEADER, you are always striving to help your people in their pursuit of God's heart. And the heart of God is right here—in the offering of grace to a lost world. Drawing closer to the heartbeat of God and His mission is what matters. Don't miss out on the opportunity to lead your congregation or Bible study into a closer relationship with God and the people He loves.

Visit www.randallhouse.com and click on the *Through the Eyes of God Leader's Guide*. In this free, on-line resource you will find teaching ideas for each chapter, a how-to guide, tips for leaders' spiritual stamina, and a personal letter from Dr. John Marshall.

To order additional copies of *Through the Eyes of God*, call 1-800-877-7030 or visit www.randallhouse.com. Call for quantity discounts.

ACKNOWLEDGMENTS

I PRAISE THE LORD for a wonderful family. They nurture me and envelope me with a cloud of acceptance.

I owe a special debt of gratitude to my secretary, Angie Roth, who joyfully typed and retyped the manuscript repeatedly.

I thank God for my wonderful church staff. Never has a pastor been surrounded by more gifted workers.

I appreciate my church family. They love their pastor, a fact that never ceases to amaze me.

I am grateful for those who took time to edit my original manuscript. Their input greatly improved this book.

Lindy Apon, Minister to Students, First Baptist Church, Russellville, Arkansas

Gary Crawford, Pastor, Westside Baptist Church, Gainesville, Florida

Amy Crider, Member, Second Baptist, Springfield, Missouri

Wayne Crull, Missouri Baptist Children's Home

Betty Doser, Member, Trinity Baptist Church,
Concord, California

John M. Edie, Minister of Adult Education/Administrator,
Second Baptist Church, Springfield, Missouri

Mike Haynes, Director of Missions, Greene County Baptist
Association, Springfield, Missouri

Jim Hill, Executive Director, Missouri Baptist Convention,
Jefferson City, Missouri

Cathy Johnson, Professor, Evangel University

Don Kammerdiener, Vice-President, International Mission
Board of the Southern Baptist Convention

Charles Marshall, Jr., Member, Garden Baptist Church,
Bridgeton, Missouri

John II and Rebekah Marshall, Author's children

Ruth Marshall, Author's wife

Dale McConnell, Consultant, Resource Services Incorporated

Pete Ramsey, Minister of Education, East Side Baptist Church,
Ft. Smith, Arkansas

Mark Thieme, Member, Second Baptist Church,
Springfield, Missouri

More Great Books
from Randall House

Regaining Balance by Randy Sawyer is a devotional journal designed to guide its readers through a season of spiritual revival. Each day of the 91-day journal encourages involvement in a handful of spiritual disciplines to help the reader regain focus and balance in every aspect of life. A free, on-line Leader's Guide allows pastors and Bible study leaders to utlize this devotional in a group setting.
ISBN 0892655186
$9.99

Minister's Manual & New Testament is an essential resource for any minister. The manual includes the entire New Testament and Psalms text as well as sample wedding services, funeral sermons, baby dedications, and much more.
ISBN 0892655402
$17.99

The Case of Stuart's Ship: A Lesson in Stewardship
by Stan Toler and Debra White Smith
Through good detective work and vivid imaginations, Stuart and Sam realize how to put stewardship into practice. This delightful book will help children of all ages understand the principles of stewardship in a fun and practical way!
ISBN 0892655348
$14.99

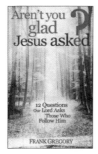

Aren't You Glad Jesus Asked?
by Frank Gregory
By focusing on 12 questions Jesus asked His disciples, this Bible study points out the importance and responsibility of evangelism in every believer's life.
ISBN 0892655410
$9.99

More Great Books
from Randall House

Handbook for Deacons
by J. D. O'Donnell
An excellent resource for deacons. The book includes the biblical basis for the origin, qualifi-cations, duties, and responsibilities of this office.
ISBN 0892650117
$8.99

I Looked for a Man and Found One
by Lorene Miley
Lorene Miley successfully thrusts her bifocals on our eyes. She allows us to see the compelling convictions, forged from God's Word and the furnace of Christian experience, which propelled her husband, LaVerne Miley from Bible College, to seminary, medical school, and the mission field.
ISBN 0892650885
$10.99

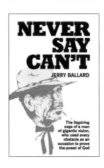

Never Say Can't by Jerry Ballard
Never Say Can't is the story of pioneer missionary, Thomas "Pop" Willey. This is the inspiring saga of a man of gigantic vision, who used every obstacle as an occasion to prove the power of God, a man whose heart beat especially for those living in the unexplored places of the earth. A realistic, intimate story of a lifelong partnership with God.
ISBN 0892650915
$12.99

Grace, Faith, Free Will by Robert E. Picirilli
Though he presents both classic Calvinism and Arminianism in order to help readers intelligently decide for themselves, Dr. Picirilli unashamedly advocates a very specific form of Arminianism as the best resolution of the tensions between the two doctrinal positions. In what he calls "Reformation Arminianism," Picirilli reclaims the original views of Arminius and his defenders.
ISBN 0892656484
$19.99

www.randallhouse.com   **800-877-7030**

Randall House commentaries

Hebrews – Outlaw	0892655143	$29.99
1,2,3 John & Revelation	0892655372	$29.99
Mark – Picirilli	0892655003	$29.99
John – Stallings	0892651377	$29.99
Romans – Forlines	0892659491	$29.99
1 & 2 Corinthians – Picirilli	0892651180	$29.99
Galatians, Colossians	0892651342	$29.99
1 Thessalonians, Philemon	0892651431	$29.99

Destination Reality *for* Teens

Within Reach - Let this issue of *Destination Reality* help your teens grasp God's goal for world missions and His desire to use them for the task. Resulting from the efforts of missions and youth expert, Paul Borthwick this edition, combines exciting activities, relevant issues, and the timelesss principles of the Word of God into a resource that leaders and learners both love!
ISBN 0892659696
Price: $19.99

www.randallhouse.com   800-877-7030

Life-Changing Curriculum

The Choice Is CLEAR

Meet CLEAR Curriculum, the Sunday School curriculum from Randall House Publications. What's so different about CLEAR learning? This exciting curriculum is based on the CLEAR Learning System™. CLEAR changes behavior as well as the knowlege of the student. With CLEAR the entire family studies the same family theme each week. From the youngest to the oldest, CLEAR makes God's Word relevant and easy-to-understand.

People around the country are choosing CLEAR curriculum because CLEAR offers exactly what they want.

- Family-Friendly Themes
- Easy-to-Use Format
- Weekly Family Links
- Timeless Biblical Truth
- Daily Devotional Studies
- Relevant Application
- Colorful, Attractive Lessons and Resources
- Emphasis on the Great Commission
- Columns by Financial Advisor, Author, and Radio Talk Show Host Dave Ramsey

CLEAR Living Magazine
(Adult)

For information
about all ages and
complete CLEAR products …
www.randallhouse.com

CLEAR Direction Student
Magazine
(Jr. High)
CLEAR Horizon Student
Magazine
(High School)

800-877-7030

Discovery Sheets (Level 2)
(Upper Elementary)
My Cuddle Time Bible Storybook
(Preschool)
Explorer's Guide (Level 1)
(Early Elementary)